Praise for The Winner's Attitude

"This book is a 'must read' for anyone who is committed to living a quality life. Warning: it could change the way you see the world!"

Barbara M. Low, RODP, SPHR
Director, MB University
MB Financial Bank

"The Winner's Attitude is a hard book to categorize—and that's a good thing. At times a spiritual development manual, at times a performance improvement workbook for customer-focused professionals and managers, it is always a challenging guide to better, fuller, and more productive living."

Patrick Canavan
Senior Vice President, Global Governance
Motorola Inc.

"A very passionately written book! With words alone accounting for only 7% of how we communicate, The Winner's Attitude will fully communicate with the billions of nerve cells inside the amazing brain. An eye-, mind-, and soul-opening experience for anyone, at any stage of their professional or personal life. This book reveals how to be passionate and in control of the winning atti   ; all."

Westby
rketing
mpany

THE WINNER'S ATTITUDE

Change How You Deal with Difficult People and
Get the Best out of Any Situation

JEFF AND VAL GEE

McGraw-Hill

New York   Chicago   San Francisco
Lisbon   London   Madrid   Mexico City
Milan   New Delhi   San Juan   Seoul
Singapore   Sydney   Toronto

1 2 3 4 5 6 7 8 9 0   AGM/AGM   0 9 8 7 6

ISBN 0-07-146764-5

McGraw-Hill books are available at special quantity discounts to use as premiums and sales promotions, or for use in corporate training programs. For more information, please write to the Director of Special Sales, Professional Publishing, McGraw-Hill, Two Penn Plaza, New York, NY 10121-2298. Or contact your local bookstore.

 This book is printed on recycled, acid-free paper containing a minimum of 50% recycled, de-inked fiber.

Library of Congress Cataloging-in-Publication Data

Gee, Jeff.
   The winner's attitude : change how you deal with difficult people and get the best out of any situation / by Jeff Gee & Val Gee.
      p. cm.
   Includes bibliographical references and index.
      ISBN 0-07-146764-5 (alk. paper)
1. Customer services. 2. Customer relations. 3. Interpersonal relations. I. Gee, Val. II. Title.
   HF5415.5.G442 2006
   658.8'12—dc22
                                        2005026804

CONTENTS

INTRODUCTION

How would it be if you could actually start to control your thoughts and your voices, so you can turn every day into an amazing day? That's what Switch will do. You don't have to spend hours rereading or trying to intellectualize it. Once you understand what's going on inside your head, you will have an amazing breakthrough that will help you in every area of your life.

Switch reminds you about how amazing you are—that no matter what is put in your way, you can overcome—not only overcome, but feel great about your day and your environment. This book is about switching on the amazing you, so that you make every day—even the mundane and routine aspects of your life—enjoyable and rewarding. It could change your life; it's that powerful.

With the help of this book, you can take a stand to go from average to outstanding. You will be able to handle not just the big problems, but the little everyday things, like the traffic, weather, family, friends, partners, the annoying colleague, or the fractious customer.

The secret to a happy life is inside your head. You never have to be at the mercy of things or people anymore to attain happiness. You have the answer within, and it is your choice to make the Attitude Switch to be the amazing you.

Chapter One

THE BRAIN SWITCH

The human brain is the last, and greatest, scientific frontier. It is truly an internal cosmos that lies contained within our skulls. The more than 100 billion nerve cells and trillion supporting cells that make up your brain and mine constitute the most elaborate structure in the known universe.

—Joel Davis
Endorphins: New Waves in Brain Chemistry

Evolving Human Beings

Switch is the twenty-first century upgrade for every evolving human being. It helps develop new pathways in the brain so you can create patterns of behavior that promote love, acceptance, peace, joy, and happiness. Switch creates a moment of choice between a stimulus and response, to a thought and action. Instead of simply reacting to the annoying and frustrating things that people say and do, Switch keeps you in the present—in the now—so you can choose to react as a human being instead of as a human animal. Switch takes you from the backseat of your life, a passenger under the control of what other people say and do, and puts you firmly in the driver's seat, where you have the power and resources to chart your own course, swerve from danger, or travel an entirely different route.

Being in control of how you react to people and events, no matter how painful or distressing, is the difference between living your life as a victim or as an enlightened human being. Switch is not about changing the people or events in your life, it is about you changing your reaction to them. It is about living your life from love instead of fear—from power instead of weakness—from acceptance instead of anger.

Many people think it's easy for others to be happy, because as an outsider it seems other people have better opportunities or are just plain lucky. They believe that if only they had the same lucky breaks in life they too would be happy—like this person who recently wrote us:

> . . . *just try getting screamed at, cursed at, things hurled at you, and called all kinds of different names from an irate customer. Also try wading through the asinine company policies that tie your hands and keep you from helping customers the way they deserve, along with a lower than you-can-live-off salary, and you have the average customer service rep and what we have to deal with every day.*

This person—let's call her Julie—feels that her problems at work far exceed those of anyone else. In her mind, no one can possibly understand what she has to deal with on a daily basis. Her viewpoint is that she has a right to be upset and frustrated with her life, essentially living her life in reaction to the influence of others. Yet we and many others we have talked to, including the rich and famous, have all experienced these events and people at one time or another. The difference is that some people, like Julie, feel victimized by it, and others don't! Some people keep moving forward to new opportunities, and others just come to a halt and get stuck in the mire. Julie has chosen to get stuck and doesn't even want to hear how to get out of the mud.

Life is a series of events—of ups and downs. You only have to look at a heart monitor screen to know that when a person is alive the line goes up and down; when they die it's flat. Sometimes life flows smoothly, everything you do and say is golden, and then something comes along and right out of the blue kicks you in the pants. And it always seems to happen just when you thought you had it all sewn up and squared away. You got the promotion, the partner, the great house, the new baby, the slim body, and then POW!—life comes along with a direct hit and you feel you're going down, spiraling out of control without a parachute or even a cushion to break the fall.

We recently gave some Super Service training to a team of customer service reps who had to give their customers two pieces of bad news: (1) prices were going up and (2) there would no longer be free delivery. Their customers, by the way, were patients who use life-saving equipment, such as dialysis machines, and who rely solely on deliveries.

After the training we went to the call center to monitor the results and were happily rewarded. The customer service reps were treating their customers in the most wonderful and caring way. One rep told us:

> I know my customers rely on me to get their syringes, needles, and machines on time and that many of them are living life and death situations. I understand they might be upset with me when I tell them the equipment has gone up in price, or they are now being charged for deliveries that used to be free. I just give them the very best service I can; it's what they deserve when they speak to me.

These customer service reps could be upset with their company for raising the prices and changing the structure of things—except they didn't get upset. They realized that it's not what happens to you—it's what you make happen with what you get that makes the difference. They chose to accept the new policies, and so when they communicated the changes to their customers, the customers listened, they empathized, and because the service reps had a positive attitude, most of their customers accepted the changes too.

Now, how do you think Julie would have handled the information from her company? She probably would have been frustrated and nervous when it came to telling her customers about the change. And more than likely, her agitation would have been picked up by her customers on the phone, who in turn are likely to get frustrated.

How you live your life is a decision—a choice that begins in your brain. Once you realize it's your choice, amazing things happen. You can choose to be at war or at peace in your life. In the moment between what someone says and your reaction to it, Switch allows you to take a different route, to fire off different synapses and leap in a new direction.

Your Three Brains

Did you know that we all have three brains? They are

- The reptilian brain
- The animal brain (also called the limbic system or mammalian brain)
- The human brain (also known as the neocortex or cerebral cortex)

In between the animal and human brain is the *Reticular Activating System*—a kind of toggle switch that resides deep inside the brain and connects to all the feelings it gets throughout the mind and body. Depending on what stimulus it receives, this switch turns on the operating system of the human or animal brain.

Using the most basic emotions—anger and love—let's look at how the switch works. If the stimulus is anger, the switch turns on the animal brain and operates from anger. If the stimulus is love, the switch turns on the human brain and operates from love. Here's the catch: many people don't realize they have a switch and spend their day flipping back and forth between the animal brain and human brain without any control over their reactions to people and events.

Let's say a person is walking down the road and someone smiles at her. This experience of love switches on her human brain, and as a result, she operates from love and smiles at people. A few blocks later someone bumps into her and gives her an angry look, maybe even curses at her. This experience of anger switches on her animal brain, and so now she is operating from anger and frustration, without even realizing why or how it happened.

Evolving humans realize that in the nanosecond between stimulus and response, they have a choice to switch: they can operate from their animal brains or their human brains. If someone sends them an angry look, they override the automatic reaction to be angry and can actually switch to their human brain and operate from love. Amazing, isn't it? Now, in order to determine which brain to operate from, you first have to understand how your three brains operate—because they all have different functions.

The Reptilian Brain

Let's start with your reptilian brain. This most ancient and primitive brain is situated at the top of your spine. To get a clear image, imagine a golf club sticking out of a golf bag. The handle is your spinal cord, and the club head is your reptilian brain sitting just at the top of the spine.

The reptilian brain is something we share with birds and reptiles and is largely unchanged by evolu-

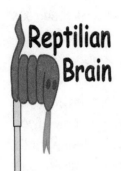

Reptilian Brain

tion. All other animals with a backbone have it because basically it keeps your body operating without you giving it a second thought. As you are probably aware, there's a lot going on in your body! You truly are a miracle. In your eyes alone there are 100 million receptors in the form of cones and rods collecting light that is sent to your brain. It is not your eyes that see—they just collect light—it is your brain that interprets your vision and sees what it wants to see. That's why some people view a situation darkly and suspiciously, while others see it happily and full of light.

Your ears have 24,000 vibrating fibers collecting sound. Again, this is sent to your brain so you can interpret what you hear. In your body there are 500 muscles, 200 bones, and 7 miles of nerve fiber. Your heart beats 36 million times a year, and there are 60,000 miles of veins, arteries, and tubing through which 600,000 gallons of blood are pumped each year—the equivalent of three Olympic-size swimming pools!

Imagine being consciously in charge of all that is going on in your body. How long do you think you would last? Probably not too long. For example, if you were in charge of your heart beating, how long would you live? Beat, beat, beat . . . I wonder what's for dinner . . . beat, beat . . . I should make a shopping list . . . beat . . . where should we go for vacation? Five minutes later you might have a shopping list and your vacation planned—except you wouldn't, you'd be dead, because you forgot to tell your heart to keep beating!

Your body is doing so much multitasking without you even being aware it. It deserves a huge prayer of gratitude every day. The reptilian brain is very important to your survival. It's like a workhorse—it just keeps going—and unless something goes wrong with your body, you don't give it a second thought.

The Animal Brain

The animal brain surrounds your reptilian brain, and it also focuses on your well-being. To visualize it, imagine a sock covering the golf club (the image we used earlier for the reptilian brain). Regardless of size, all animals have an animal brain—and we, the human animal, are no different. The animal brain is about one thing and one thing only: SURVIVAL! It is born in fear, lives in fear, and dies in fear. Its job is to keep us alive and out of danger. Watch an animal documentary and you'll notice that every animal is on alert—afraid they may end up as lunch for another animal.

Sometimes during a workshop someone will raise their hand and say, "My pet is different. My pet loves me! My pet doesn't live in fear!"

We agree, and then ask, "Do you feed your pet, love your pet, and treat your pet kindly?"

They say, "Yes, of course."

We ask, "If you didn't feed your pet and treated it unkindly, would your pet still love you?"

After a moment, they realize, "Maybe not!"

We talk about how pets seem different from wild animals because they're domesticated. They can appear so human we even give them "people" names and talk to them like they're human beings. And as long as we treat our pets well—they go along with it. A pet that has its survival taken care of in terms of food, sleep, and well-being, is docile, domesticated, and fun to be with. If it feels threatened, however, the animal brain kicks in and it suddenly becomes a fearful, barking, snarling, biting creature.

In packs, even domesticated animals can be aggressive. A lovely little house dog can leave its home, join up with other neighborhood dogs, and go on the prowl and even attack people. Not that your pet would ever do that—because you keep it leashed and disciplined—we're talking about pet owners who don't take responsibility for their pets.

And although animals sleep a lot, have you noticed that they are always on alert? A few years ago we had a beautiful bulldog called Millie, and sometimes we would sneak up on her to see if she ever truly slept. We would always get so far, and when we were just a couple of feet away, Millie would open one eye and look up as if to say, "Hey, you think you can sneak up on me—you got another think coming!"

Clearly, the animal brain survival mechanism is very handy if you're out late at night in a strange neighborhood. It checks things out so that if danger occurs you can stay and fight, or run for your life. This "fight or flight" mechanism, originally discovered by Harvard physiologist Walter Cannon, is a response system hard-wired into our animal brain to protect us from bodily harm.

Because the animal brain is all about survival, its job is to look for any little thing that seems out of place or odd—even in safe situations like the workplace or at home. The problem is, if the animal brain takes over, that's all it looks for. Like bodyguards who watch over VIPs, everything is classified as a potential danger—everything is alarming and a possible threat—it has to be that way for them to do their job properly.

Although most of us are not bodyguards, we still operate from the animal brain as if we were. So if another person smiles or gives a compliment, the animal brain automatically thinks, "Why is that person smiling at me? They must want something! Better watch out!"

The animal brain makes a terrible master because it only has one place to come from—fear. If your animal brain is in charge, you live in constant fear for your survival. Now, if you are in charge of your animal brain, you're in great shape because you are in control, can decide what is dangerous and what is not—you can act appropriately.

Switch is about you being in charge of your animal brain so that when it's a sunny day, for instance, you can enjoy it instead of being worried or fearful. We live in Chicago, where the temperature is extremely hot in the summer and very cold in the winter. We've noticed, and perhaps you have too, that people who complain about the heat during the summer are the same ones who bundle up, hunched over, in the winter, saying, "It's too cold." That's the animal brain in operation—it can never relax long enough to enjoy the moment.

The animal brain is always on the lookout to make sure it is not being taken advantage of, and it will document things people say, just to "get them" later. It will sue people even if the mistake was a legitimate one. Like the story we heard just yesterday about a man who had stomach pains in the middle of the night. He went to the emergency room and was told nothing was wrong. The next morning he went to his own doctor, who discovered he had a burst appendix and was suffering from peritonitis. He was rushed to the hospital, seriously ill. Fortunately, the hospital treated him and he recovered.

Then he decided to sue them for making the mistake in the first place.

Now I agree with some of you who may be thinking, "Right, he should sue! They made a wrongful diagnosis and he could have died." Except he didn't die—he could have, but he didn't. And if he sues, who pays? We do. The animal brain doesn't care about that, though; the animal brain is into survival and nothing else. It doesn't care about community, about accepting that we all make mistakes, even doctors. It isn't grateful for being alive, because it lives so much in fear of death and being taken advantage of.

The above scenario is the animal brain's approach to everything. Whether it is a relationship between friends, married couples, countries, customers, companies, or employees—when people operate from their animal brains they live in fear and will do anything to survive.

You may be thinking, "When I talk to so and so I have to be in my animal brain because they're out to get me." Or, "When I talk to a certain coworker, I just can't help getting annoyed." Well, that's one way to look at it—remember, two people operating from their animal brains can only create fight or flight situations.

Because the animal brain operates from fear, it has to live in an environment of fear, and it will do anything to create it. It will remind you about things you did in the past so that you feel guilty and bad. It will remind you of things other people did to you in the past that hurt you. It will nag you about things in the future so that you feel worried and uncertain about tomorrow. When people operate from their animal brains, relationships and situations become complicated, difficult, and messy. Living with guilt, people will literally give themselves a life sentence of feeling bad.

So what can you do about it? How can you ensure that you don't operate from the animal brain? There are two simple steps:

1. Realize you are operating from the animal brain.

2. Switch to your human brain.

If, for example, you realize you're being mean to someone, you switch and begin to show kindness. If you're being angry with a person, you switch and begin to listen to his needs.

Now, if feeling guilty created a better you—it would be a different story. All guilt does, however, is make you feel guiltier. Guilt leads to feeling depressed, looking at the past, etc. The key is to remember that the past is the past, and what you did back then you would not do now because you have new information. When guilty or angry feelings come up, that's when you have the opportunity to switch. Look at what's making you feel that way, and figure out how to switch out of the animal brain and into the human brain.

One of the problems about operating from the animal brain is that often you don't even realize you're doing it! Because the animal brain operates from fear, it is too busy surviving to be objective. So, in Table 1.1 you'll see a list of feelings and emotions that can only be activated from your animal brain. If you find yourself feeling any of the following emotions, you instantly know that you are operating from your animal brain, and you can then make the choice to stay in it or switch. It's your life and your choice! We call them Animal Brain Igniters because they literally fire up your animal brain.

Animal Brain Igniters

If you are having any thoughts, feelings, or actions associated with the words in Table 1.1, you are operating from your animal brain.

Critical	Prideful	Frustrated
Judgmental	Greedy	Bored
Angry	Belligerent	Righteous
Upset	Grasping	Envious
Depressed	Worrying	Uncertain
Embarrassed	Lying	Superior
Pompous	Selfish	Resentful
Suspicious	Possessive	Cruel
Arrogant	Jealous	Guilty
Destructive	Irritable	Boastful

Table 1.1

BRAIN SWITCH EXERCISE

When you find yourself operating from your animal brain and want to switch to your human brain, use the following exercise:

1. Take a deep breath.

2. As you breathe out, let the negative feeling go.

3. Switch to your human brain.

4. Breathe in *love, peace, acceptance.*

SWITCH TEASER

What do you know about your three brains? Circle T for True or F for False for each of the following questions.

1. The reptilian brain is the most primitive brain.　　T　F

2. Every human being has just one brain.　　T　F

3. The reptilian brain monitors body functions.　　T　F

SWITCH TEASER (CONT.)

4. The animal brain is born in fear. T F

5. The animal brain is about survival. T F

Check your answers. Five correct answers means that you understand how your reptilian and animal brains work. Good job! Less than three and you may want to reread the chapter again—of course your animal brain will say you don't need to because it hates being told what to do.

Switch Teaser Answers: 1.T, 2.F, 3.T, 4.T, 5.T

The Human Brain

Fortunately for us human beings, we have evolved a human brain that surrounds the animal brain. This is what makes us operate from love, acceptance, peace, and understanding. It's the brain that allows us to share, help a coworker, volunteer, and respect and honor other people. As for its location, visualize it as a helmet on top of the sock we depicted earlier as your animal brain.

The human brain is different from the animal brain because it operates not from the dark and low level of fear and survival, but from a higher level. It is born in love, lives in love, and dies in love. If that sounds too hokey for you, just look around—there are millions of stories about ordinary people doing extraordinary things just for the sheer joy of doing them.

Consider, as just one example among many, the outpouring of relief funds that went to the tsunami disaster areas. From large government funds to the six-year-old boy in Shenyang, China, who donated his life savings of $22. Or the citizens of Sweden, a country of 9 million inhabitants, who raised more than $70 million, while struggling to cope with the fact that almost 2,000 of their compatriots went missing in the tragedy.

And yes, you could say that in times of tragedy people automatically rally round, and that they don't behave like that in their ordinary, everyday lives. Well, let's look at that. In fact, there are plenty of stories about ordinary people operating from their human brain and doing extraordinary things—every day of their lives.

Like a friend of ours who runs an adoption agency and regularly goes to China to adopt baby girls. He doesn't do this because it will make him lots of money or because it is a comfortable existence—he has to hold fund-raising events all the time to have enough money for the agency. So why is he doing it? Because he is coming from his human brain—he wants to work at a job that is both satisfying to him and rewarding to others.

Or the woman who supports young people who want to become actors. In her spare time she helps them write, rehearse, and put on performances for friends, family, and the local community. She too has to organize fund-raisers for money to help these kids. Again, she is someone who operates from her human brain.

Or another friend of ours who goes to a children's hospital to comfort babies with AIDS, because otherwise they would never get held.

No doubt you know people like the friends of ours who donate time to help adults read and write, or know or have heard about those who volunteer their time to take senior citizens shopping for groceries once a week.

In fact, Jeff himself is an example, having volunteered at a small school for children with autism and other problems. He enjoyed working with the kids and formed relationships with some of them. Then his schedule got so crazy that he was often away and couldn't keep to the kind of consistency the kids needed. Finally, it got to be more of a problem for the school and staff to have him volunteer than not, so now he volunteers time to coach people via the telephone, which he can do more easily.

Volunteering is about having the time to do something for other people without jeopardizing your life or the people in it. It doesn't make sense volunteering for a good cause outside your home if the people inside your home need help. And lots of people are doing just that—quietly going about their lives in a way that is worthy of being called a warrior, like Janice.

Janice came to one of our Switch seminars, and in the course of that day we learned that she was a single mother who lived one hour by car from where she worked. Except she didn't have a car, so she had to take a taxi to the train station and then hop on a bus after her train ride to get to work, which was in fact a two-hour trip. She got up at 4:30 a.m. every morning, took care of her children, then left for work.

We asked her, "Why do you do it?"

"I have to take care of my children and this is the best job I could get," she replied.

Ordinary people doing extraordinary things. And the most amazing thing about Janice is that she was great all the way through the seminar. She was the best participant, laughing, smiling, answering questions, always focused and involved. She is volunteering right inside her own life—taking action and doing the things necessary for the well-being of herself and her kids.

Not everyone is this way. Some people have cars, live only a few minutes from where they work, and still aren't happy. Delia, another participant in a Switch seminar, said, "I'm not going to affirm my day." That's one of the things we ask people to do—to "affirm" their day in the morning. It only takes a couple of seconds. When we asked her why, she said, "I would feel stupid standing in front of a mirror and affirming my day."

Remember what the animal brain is about? Survival. And how do animals survive? They hide. If you take a walk through a wooded place, you'll notice you don't often see any animals. Do you think that's because there aren't any? No, it's because they're hiding because they are afraid of you.

So of course when we operate from our animal brain, we too go into hiding; we don't want to be seen. But here's the amazing thing: Delia didn't even want to be seen by *herself*. Standing in front of a mirror and looking at herself—she wouldn't do it. She was one that got away. Or maybe not . . . her coworkers told us later that they still held out hope she would get to Switch. We hope so, because Delia operating from her human brain is a very sweet lady with lots of knowledge and lots to give.

There are many more people we know doing extraordinary things for their communities. Like the woman in one Switch seminar whose 26-year-old son had become a paraplegic through a motorbike accident. She now cares for him at her home and holds down a full-time job to help pay for his medication. She said, "The first time I sent him off to the pharmacy, I was very nervous because he had two roads to cross in his wheelchair. But the next day the lady at the pharmacy told me, 'Your son came in by himself yesterday. He is amazing.'" And he is. Can you imagine having the courage to cross a road in a wheelchair operated by one finger of one hand?

What Does It Mean to Be Human?

In Switch seminars we ask people, "If an alien visited from another planet, how would you demonstrate the creativity and power of human beings? What would you show them? Where would you take them?"

Immediately people answer with a list: museums, art galleries, philharmonic orchestras, skyscrapers, books about people who have climbed Mount Everest, stories about people who've sailed round the world single-handed, about people who've rescued strangers from burning buildings, about mathematicians, physicists, hospitals, and on and on.

Every day millions upon millions of people achieve extraordinary things, yet what do we mostly hear about in the news and media? Guns, shootings, chaos, wars, bankruptcies, tax fraud, drugs, prostitution, mass murder, and so on. Just today on the news we heard of more terrorist bombings in London. We have nephews and nieces who live and work in London, so of course we called our family. Fortunately, no one in our family was hurt—our nephew was late to work that morning, otherwise he would have been on one of the trains that got blown up. My brother said, "They take so many precautions—they've removed garbage cans from the underground tube stations—they'll probably start issuing plastic ID cards soon." Then he went on to say, "It's ironic that yesterday we were celebrating that the Olympics are going to be held in London—and now this!"

Given what you know now about the animal brain and the human brain, which brain do you think the people are in when they commit these kinds of crimes? That's right, the animal brain. The animal brain lives in fear and survival, and that's the environment it wants to create. It doesn't know anything else—so even if the person belongs to a particular religion that speaks of love, acceptance, peace, and understanding, the animal brain will override those teachings and devise a plan to spread fear, chaos, and destruction. We're right and they're wrong, and the end justifies the means.

There are probably more stories about people doing amazing things per capita than people doing ghastly things, so why are we bombarded with the horrid details of what the human animal is creating? Because the human animal is so easy to engage—it loves intrigue, gossip, and bad things happening to other people—and then it feels safe. Remember, it's all about survival: "Ah! I survived another day unlike those other people who didn't. Thank you, thank you, thank you!"

The Golden Rule

In the animal brain there are sides and positions to hold. In the human brain there is connectedness and the Golden Rule: "Treat others as you would have them treat you." The human animal is consumed with survival at any costs. The human being wants to love and be loved.

The Golden Rule doesn't say "you have to believe in the same things that I believe in" or "you have to have the same color of skin that I do" or "you have to come from the same land or have the same kind of education or history." The Golden Rule simply states, "Treat others as you would like to be treated." So how would you like to be treated? Here is a clue: whether you are a customer, coworker, spouse, son, daughter, parent, friend, or stranger, you want one main thing, and that is love.

If you love someone, you do things that are for their highest good. If you love your neighbors and treat them like your own family members, you don't do things that will annoy them. For example, a neighbor of ours doesn't like us to park opposite his driveway. The previous owner of our home had a running battle with him, but we don't because we've spoken to him and now ask our friends not to park opposite his driveway. Why create battles with neighbors? It just leads to misery and upset—no one wins.

Human Brain Igniters

The list of emotions, feelings, and actions in Table 1.2 can only be activated when you are in the human brain. A good way of affirming that you are in fact operating from your human brain is to recognize when the words in the table are describing you. This is why we call them "Human Brain Igniters."

Loving	Optimistic	Powerful
Giving	Purposeful	Helpful
Accepting	Considerate	Humorous
Truthful	Gentle	Joyful
Tolerant	Trusting	Energetic
Take action	Spontaneous	Encouraging
Concerned	Inspired	Generous
Appreciative	Thoughtful	Modest
Reliable	Honest	Patient
Open	Peaceful	Warm

Table 1.2

BRAIN SWITCH EXERCISE

The following exercise is a great way of keeping your human brain switched on and fully operational. Any time you need reminding that you are an amazing human being, take the following steps:

BRAIN SWITCH EXERCISE (CONT.)

1. From the previous list, circle the one word that for you stands out from the others.

2. Breathe in deeply and silently repeat, "I am _____." (Repeat the word you circled.)

3. Feel the experience of the word circulate throughout your mind, body, and spirit.

4. Repeat as often as necessary.

SWITCH TEASER

What do you know about your human brain? Circle T for True or F for False for each of the following questions.

1. Ordinary people seldom do amazing things.   T   F

2. Affirming your day takes just seconds.   T   F

3. The human brain loves intrigue and gossip.   T   F

SWITCH TEASER (CONT.)

4. The human brain is born in love,   T   F
lives in love, and dies in love.

5. It is not important to switch to   T   F
the human brain.

Check your answers below. Five correct answers means that you understand your human brain— good job! Less than four and you may want to reread the chapter again—your human brain will support you.

Switch Teaser Answers: 1.F 2.T 3.F 4.T 5.F

Human beings create amazing things because of the human brain. All we need to do is *activate* it, and that's where the switch comes in.

The Reticular Activating System

It's great to have all this brainpower, and the switch inside your head that controls it all, as we said earlier, is the Reticular Activating System.

For those of you who enjoy scientific explanations, the Reticular Activating System is a complex collection of neurons that serve as a point of convergence for signals from the external world and from your interior environment. In other words, it is the part of your brain where the world outside of you meets the world inside and connects with your thoughts and feelings.

This switch is responsible for you being conscious and paying attention. It runs all the way up to the center of the brain and connects with your emotions and feelings.

For people who don't realize they have a switch that controls their operating system (the three brains), it can be like operating with a faulty circuit. If you've ever had your cable go out, that's what it's like inside your head. Let's say you're driving to work. You know the route well and you're on autopilot. Suddenly a car cuts in front of you: the outer world has impacted your inner world. If you are not in control of your switch, you'll go back and forth between the animal brain and the human brain—between feelings of rage and logic—until the strongest one wins and you either calm down or flip out.

For some people, it's a choice they make. Like our friend Steve, who seems to enjoy getting frustrated with other car drivers and makes a game of it. "It's the one place where I can legitimately blow off steam," he told us. Not that Steve has road rage and drives like a maniac, tailgating and hurling abuse. His reactions while driving are more in the line of "I can't believe that person just did that" or "I just don't get it. This is a straight three-lane highway that goes for hundreds of miles. How can we be slowed down to a halt? We should all be able to drive at the same speed!" His (whimsical) solution was, "I wish there were helicopters with giant magnets attached so they could pick up the cars causing the problem and put them by the side of the road so we could all get past." Now, if Steve ever starts saying these things without the humor in his voice, it would be time to get worried. That's because the animal brain doesn't have a sense of humor!

We Are Still Evolving

People who operate their switch have a sense of their own well-being, an awareness of how they want to be. And even if they don't always make the switch as often as they would like, they still know that they're in charge. They take responsibility for their actions.

We are still in the midst of evolving and learning about Switch. As we evolve from human animal into human being you will see miracles happen. People you believed were nasty and rude will become warm and loving. Situations and relationships you thought were irrevocably destroyed will become renewed and energized. And it will happen because you made the switch. Here's what a couple of people have said about it:

> *The teachings are full of promise and enthusiasm. The new way of thinking and looking at things are believable. The habits I have formed are, however, a bit resistant still. Each day is a little life, and now I'm living with a more deliberate style.*

> *I am being amazing! And to make sure, I'm asking myself just that in the mirror every morning. I've noticed I feel more comfortable doing it now that it's repetitive. Thank you for an eye-, mind-, and soul-opening experience!*

Switch is about you becoming the human being you have always wanted to be. This is your opportunity—it doesn't get any easier to wait and do it later, it just gets later. And here's another AMAZING thing:

because so many global organizations have already made the switch, you are not alone. More and more you will meet and communicate with people who are also making the switch to evolve into more of a human being and less of a human animal.

Corporations Spread Switch Worldwide

Switch has been embraced by Fortune 500 companies all over America, and inspired by the results, they have taken it to their offices in Costa Rica, India, Australia, England, Holland, Poland, Brazil, Mexico, Argentina, Singapore, Japan, Manila, Jakarta, and South Korea.

We have received numerous e-mails concerning how Switch effects people at work. Here's one of them:

> Hola! Ninety-eight percent of the time I affirm my day—which in the past I did not. I am getting better—I catch myself when I drop off. I am being amazing and I remember that every second I can make a difference and only I can do it for myself, even more so when the animal would like to come

*out! I will be patient and understanding so every-
one can see that I am in my human brain. I realize
we all have the human part of us and forgot how to
properly use it. I never realized that we tend to let
the animal take over most of the time when all we
need is to allow the human to take more control
instead of the animal!*

Switch does not mean that our life suddenly
becomes all blue skies and blooming roses—it's realizing that we have a choice. We do not have to be
influenced by a dull day or a dull companion—we
decide: animal brain or human brain? Like this next
e-mail:

*I have been feeling sick and under the weather all
week, yet I've emerged being as productive and as
helpful to my customers as I could be, especially by
showing up for work even when I didn't feel like it
and to serve others and be there for my customers.
Everyone, and especially myself, seems to be working with a renewed attitude and a fresh perspective
since learning about Switch. One of the biggest
things I got from the seminar is how important it is
to be great for our internal customers, since in this
company there is a tremendous reliance upon team-
work. I have been affirming myself every day for*

> *my customers, making sure "my job" doesn't get in*
> *the way of the needs of my customers.*

When you switch, people around you automatically switch too. It just takes one, and then one more, and pretty soon everyone has switched. Like Barbara, a working mom who discovered the following attending our seminar:

> *I was standing in the bathroom affirming my day,*
> *and my seven-year-old daughter said to me, "Can*
> *I do that Mom?" I told her, "Sure you can, honey."*
> *Now we affirm our day together every morning,*
> *and it has made such a difference to our relation-*
> *ship, to her grades, and just to our sense of well-*
> *being as a family.*

And sometimes it takes a lot of hard work, as noted in this e-mail we received from a company that had three CEOs in as many years and was continually going through change:

> *First of all I want to tell you that your seminar is*
> *the BEST I have ever attended . . . We all came*
> *back highly motivated, and I think a lot of us did*
> *affirm our day and I believe it worked for several*
> *days, but then it changed. The animal has taken*
> *full control and we now travel in packs. The human*

being is being eaten alive. Our management is very inflexible and it is my way or the highway. They make the rules and we have no input. Plus, we do not have the resources we need for review, things are so backlogged that hopes of ever catching up seems impossible, and when all is said and done it is really the customer who is suffering.

We are told to work as one company, work as a team and become the employer of choice. Right now I feel as if those are just words, and that the team concept has already fallen by the wayside. It is more like a dictatorship. I think I really used this e-mail to vent. I did also receive an e-mail from a former coworker who has been in two years of therapy after working for this company. Actually, a lot of us thought maybe we could get a corporate rate if we went to her therapist. On a lighter side, HAVE A GREAT DAY! And I will do my best to affirm my day and move on, one day at a time. My dream is to own a hot dog stand on the beach and make other people happy with good food and the best customer service.

In this e-mail you can actually "see" the animal brain and the human brain in action. It started out from the human brain, then went into animal brain survival and fear talk, and finally ended with the human brain and a little bit of humor about the therapist and the hot dog stand.

Keep in mind that Switch will not change the events that occur in your working life. It's not about that. Companies are going to decide the way they do things and managers will dictate the rules. It would be nice if managers asked us for input, but too often they don't because—guess what?—the boss isn't asking for the managers' input either.

Then there are the e-mails like this next one from John, who recently told us:

I never really appreciated my wife until I made the switch. Now I take her coffee in the morning, and boy, just that one little thing has changed our whole relationship.

And Amy, who said:

I have this employee called Edward. He never looks people in the eye and all he does is complain. Then he made the switch and became a completely different person. Now he looks up and says good morning. If he has a problem, he asks for help. Everyone in the department has noticed the difference—it's amazing!

Or the manager who commented:

I just realized, this is a life thing, isn't it? We're teaching people about how to live their lives—not just inside work, but at home too.

One final point and then we will get on with the process of helping you make the switch. I once read that only 5 percent of people ever finish a book. As an evolving human being, take the time to read this one to the end. Keep it around and "dip" into it from time to time. The secrets of Switch abound throughout the book, so don't miss out on your opportunity to switch—read it all. You deserve it! You are an amazing human being, after all.

No One Can Do It for You

Wouldn't it be great if you could pay someone else to work out for you? Put your order in: "Today I would like you to do 100 push-ups, 20 sit-ups, and half an hour on the treadmill. Oh, and can you do some weight lifting—arms today, please—three sets of 12 reps using 15 pounds. You can work on legs tomorrow."

How much would you pay someone to work out for you? What would it be worth to have a fit, healthy body? Maybe you do have one. Maybe you have that part of your life handled and what you need help with is a relationship you have. How much would you pay someone to step in for you and make it work? Someone to whom you would say, "Okay, today I need some time off to be alone. My significant other has been complaining that we don't go out enough so I want you to step in for me. Book a nice restaurant and spend $100. There's a movie out that my honey wants to go see. It doesn't interest me in the slightest, so maybe you can go do that afterward. Now here are some ground rules: You can listen and discuss things—and if you talk about anything really important, take notes. You can hold hands—that's it. Oh, and make sure you're back no later than 11 p.m." It sounds ridiculous, doesn't it? Yet how many times have you not wanted to do something that your beloved one has wanted to do, and you persuaded her not to do it. Or maybe you didn't even persuade her. Maybe you just plain said, "No! I'm not doing that."

And if the truth be known, if another person stepped in right at that moment and said, "I'll go with her—you stay here, don't worry—we'll have lots of fun," you would hate it. Many people want to have a great relationship, except they forget that there is another person involved with a whole different agenda from theirs.

When Two Brains Communicate

In a relationship between two people there are at least four points of view involved. There is your animal brain, her animal brain, your human brain, and her human brain. Now if your two human brains are in communication with each other—your relationship will work, PERIOD!

If your two animal brains are in communication, good luck! Here's why: the animal brain doesn't care if it works or not. Remember, your animal brain is about survival at any cost—even the cost of your relationship! If two people are both operating from their animal brains, it quickly gets into fight or flight. Nobody wins and everyone loses, especially if kids are involved.

"Oh great, Mom and Dad are at it again. I suppose that's what being married looks like. I'm never going to do it."

And what about work? Would you pay someone to go to work for you so you could stay home and catch up on your sleep or your household chores? What if she did a better job than you and your boss hired her and gave you the heave-ho? Would you be happy then?

Or what about winning the lottery? Then you wouldn't have to go to work ever again. You could even pay other people to come work for you. Would that make you happy? It seems most people who win the lottery aren't actually any happier. In fact, there are lots of stories of people who turn to alcohol, get divorced, or spend all their money and end up worse off than before.

Happiness Is Right Now

You can be happy right now, today, doing whatever it is that you are doing—even if you hate it, you can be happy. It all comes down to making a switch. Do you want to switch on your human brain and motivate yourself to be happy, or do you want to switch it off and be miserable?

If you believed all the advertising on TV, you would think the average human being is depressed, suffers from heartburn, sexual dysfunction, and is grossly overweight. Do you ever see anyone advertising the Switch? This is what the instructions for an ad about switching to the human brain would look like: Camera zooms in to a person doing laundry, smiling and saying, "Isn't it great! All I have to do is put my dirty stuff in this machine, add a bit of detergent, and BOOM, 20 minutes later it's done. Then all I have to do is take it out and put it in the dryer." Then the person would get all serious, look directly into the camera and say, "I used to not like doing laundry. Then I learned how to switch to my human brain and my whole point of view changed."

Or there's a person sitting in front of a huge table laden with food. They choose meat, vegetables, and fruit while looking right into the camera and saying, "I used to have indigestion real bad, and then one day I realized I am in charge of what I eat." And in the next shot you see them playing tennis and having a great time, and just as the ball lands in their court, they say, "It's all a choice to switch."

Except no one is going to pay for that kind of advertising, because there's nothing to sell and nothing to buy. No one cares if you feel happy or not. In fact, if you are in charge of your switch, who benefits? You do.

The Animal Brain Travels in Packs

Sometimes people form animal brain packs. Sally, a friend of ours, told us, "It was one of my first jobs and we processed forms like a conveyor belt. I was really excited about getting the job, so I worked really hard my first day. The next day, one of the people who had been working there a long time said to me, 'You don't have to work so hard, Sally, you make the rest of us look like we're not doing a good job.' I couldn't believe it. My parents always told me to work hard, and here was this older person telling me I was working too hard! I didn't stay there long. I didn't want to end up looking like the rest of them—miserable and unhappy."

Your First Day at Work

Can you remember your first day at work? We ask people in our seminar this question, and after a bit of prompting someone will finally raise her hand and say, "Yes, I remember my first day." Then we ask her how she prepared the night before, and she says, "The night before I had all my clothes laid out, and I even got up *before* the alarm. I got to work half an hour before I needed to."

Then we inquire about how she reacted when someone asked her to do something, and she says, "I would walk quickly over and find out what the individual wanted me to do."

In the seminar, the group laughs because they recognize this reaction and know they felt similarly on their first day. Then we ask how they were after they'd been at work for a few weeks, and again everyone in the group laughs, because they know they were completely changed. They hit the snooze button because they knew it took them exactly 40 minutes from getting out of bed to arriving at work. And they made it just about on time, and if someone asked them to do something, they were more likely to reply, "I'll be there in a minute. I just have to finish this first."

What happened? What is the difference between your first day at work and your second, third, or five hundredth day?

Your switch. That's the difference. You decided that you know everything there is to know about your job, your coworkers, your customers, your prospects, your product, your services, and your competition. And you know what happens when you "know" something? When you become "familiar" with something? You switch off.

When You Switch Off

You switch off and you stop being in charge of your human brain. The animal brain takes over and now you're asleep. Not literally sleeping on the job, although maybe you have the kind of job where you can do that. No, this is not about physically sleeping, although it resembles sleeping because when you're in your animal brain, pretty much everything in your consciousness is turned off and your animal brain puts on the remote control.

Can you imagine all the time and money that goes into hiring people? Some places have extensive testing procedures that people pass because they have their human brains switched on. The company hires them, and for the first few weeks they are a delight to work with. Coworkers appreciate them, the boss is pleased, and customers are happy. Then one day their animal brains turn up for work. "What the heck happened? He's always late. And that report he was supposed to do—I've been waiting days for it. I even had a complaint about him from a customer yesterday. I think I'm going to send him a first warning letter."

When the employee gets the letter, one of two things happen. He makes the switch back to his human brain and remembers that he really wanted this job and that if he loses it, it will be hard to get another one that pays as well. Or his animal brain digs its heels in and he takes umbrage: "A warning letter! I do my job. I was only late once last week. And that customer was definitely wrong . . ." And on and on and on.

This is because the animal brain justifies everything. Just look at the most extreme cases, that of dictators of the past and today who rule by fear and justify the most horrendous acts of violence in their countries, including killing, torture, and starvation.

Switch is about making the choice to be in your animal brain or your human brain. To evolve into a human being or stay stuck as a human animal.

You Only See What You're Looking For

Switch decides which brain you choose to operate from. It's the place where your external world meets your internal world.

Have you ever bought a car? We bought one recently—a classy silver model about which we said,

"Wow, this is amazing, the perfect car for us." We hadn't seen anything like it. It was definitely one of a kind.

Guess what happened moments after we had driven it off the lot? You guessed it. We saw exactly the same car in front of us. Over the next few days we saw them everywhere. How come? How come we hadn't noticed the car before? Well, here's the answer— you only see what you're looking for.

It's the same when you're in love. Everywhere you look, people are holding hands, kissing, and laughing together. How come? It's because you see what you're looking for. When you're in love, that's what you see.

When people are in hate, on the other hand, all they see is a dark depressing world with people scowling and looking angry. Why? Because you see what you're looking for.

Everything that you smell, see, touch, hear, and feel from your external world triggers either the human or the animal brain. If it triggers the animal brain, you will respond with fear. If it triggers the human brain, you will respond with love. The problem is, because you see what you're looking for, even if you walk into the most beautiful place in the world, if you perceive the world from a negative point of view, you'll automatically trigger your animal brain and see something else, entirely overlooking the place's beauty.

You can get trapped in a cycle: the world looks positive or negative depending on what you look for, and that reinforces the animal or human brain, which depends on the brain you most habitually choose to operate from. It's like being on one of those little hamster wheels: you can only get off when you are in charge of your switch.

When you choose to switch to a positive point of view, your entire world—both external and internal— will change. How did Nelson Mandela create a garden within the prison compound? He first had to have a vision of flowers. How did Michael Jordan become an all-time great basketball player? He spent time envisioning every shot before he stepped onto the court. How did Mother Teresa see the beauty in everyone? That is what she wanted to see.

What Signals Are You Sending?

What are you looking for in your life? What kind of world do you see? Do you see a positive world or a negative world?

We're not suggesting that you live in a Mary Poppins world where everything is roses, blue skies, and happy people, a world where there are no murders, rapes, or war. You can still be aware of those things if you want to by reading or listening to the news. It's just that with Switch, you see them from a different point of view. Instead of getting upset by terrorists, for example, and giving terrorists energy by getting depressed and fearful, make the decision to stop being a terrorist in your own life.

Stop spreading anxiety, worry, gossip, lies, and negative thoughts and start spreading hope, peace, joy, compliments, and positive thoughts. The most effective way of destroying a terrorist attack is by being happy. As our Founding Fathers put it: "Life, Liberty, and the Pursuit of Happiness." Don't allow a few desperate individuals to take away your peace of mind. Don't allow the human animals of the world to create more human animals. Our job is to evolve into human beings.

Forgiveness Is Key

Part of evolving into a human being is to be forgiving. First forgive yourself and then forgive others. Start with your parents. If you have any kind of problem with them, now is the time to forgive and forget. Then work outward with your family—siblings, aunts, uncles, grandparents. Then your friends, coworkers, customers, bosses, employers, people from other countries. I remember my grandmother's reaction after World War II whenever someone walked into the room who was from the "opposite side": she would walk out. Even long after the war was over—without even knowing if this person had been in the resistance and actually helped "her side" during the war!—she would walk out.

Holding grudges only hurts the one who holds the grudge. So if you hold a grudge against anyone, remember that she didn't know any better. If she did know better, she wouldn't have done those things, whatever those things were. Stop war by getting off the warring path and onto the path of forgiveness.

By the way, forgiving individuals doesn't mean you condone what they did or did not do. Forgiveness is merely saying, "I forgive you." No questions asked. Also, you can forgive others without even seeing or talking with them. You just do it in your heart and say, "I forgive you." On some other level they will know.

We told you at the beginning of the book to expect miracles. When you switch on your human brain and become an evolving human being, miracles do happen. Here are some Brain Switchers that will help you switch to your human brain.

BRAIN SWITCHERS

You know when you have made a switch to the human brain when you

Feel good about yourself.

See the good in others.

Are willing to forgive.

Help and give to others.

Leave a place better than you found it.

Laugh a lot.

Clean up after yourself and others.

Are pleasant and pleasing to be with.

See things as they are and remain detached.

Keep an objective outlook.

Don't take things personally.

Never buy into failure.

See death as another journey.

BRAIN SWITCHERS (CONT.)

Fear not.

Love thy neighbor as thyself.

Act more and talk less.

Walk your talk or don't say anything.

Smile a lot.

Sing in the shower.

Treat others as you would like to be treated.

Treat yourself well.

Are kind to yourself and others.

Make healthy food choices.

Exercise.

Support yourself and others in being great.

Reward yourself for doing a great job.

Reward others for doing a great job.

Make your bed in the morning.

Clean your closets.

Keep your home clean.

Hum if you can't whistle; whistle if you can't sing.

BRAIN SWITCHERS (CONT.)

Are a positive influence.

Recycle.

Are open to realizations.

Are a joyful participant in everything you do.

Spread love and peace.

SWITCH TEASER

What do you know about Switch? Circle T for True or F for False for each of the following questions.

1. The Reticular Activating System turns on the human or animal brain.   T   F

2. We call Switch the operating system of your brain.   T   F

3. Switching on your human brain is your choice.   T   F

4. Switching on your animal brain is your choice.   T   F

5. Once you know about Switch, you always have a choice.   T   F

SWITCH TEASER (CONT.)

Check your answers below. Five correct answers means that you understand your switch—good job! Less than four and you may want to reread the chapter again—you are in charge of gaining knowledge.

Switch Teaser Answers: 1.T, 2.T, 3.T, 4.T, 5.T

Free Switch Bonuses

Download your free Switch bonuses—screensaver, newsletter, and tips on how to create a healthy, wealthy, happy, and successful life—at www.mjlearn ing.com/book/switch.

Chapter Two

OVERCOME
YOUR ANGER

If you take a Cray computer (one of the largest computers in the world) and measure its wiring, it has about 60,000 miles in total. If you take the brain and look at it in those terms, it has been estimated that it has over 200,000 miles of wiring!

—Tony Buzan
Make the Most of Your Mind

There is a lot of heat around the word *anger*. It's as if the word itself has an energy to it that creates fear and anguish! Well, anger is created in the animal brain, so it makes sense that it creates fear. So the first way to deal with anger is to not be afraid of it. That's right—stop being scared of anger. Look at it for what it is. For example, I woke up the other morning and felt angry about something someone had done. It was a silly, inconsequential thing and I was definitely in my animal brain about it. I wanted to switch to my human brain and couldn't get beyond the anger I felt. So I decided to tell the truth about my anger. I listed in my head everything I was angry about with this person.

In retrospect it was funny. There I was, writing a book about Switch, unable to switch myself because of all my anger. I listed about 30 things; some were a stretch, yet I wanted to get everything out. By the end of the list I did feel lighter because I had switched, and then something miraculous happened. I realized that I was all of those things that I'd listed. I was lazy, I was mean, I was this, that, and the other. When I switched, instead of being angry at the person, I realized all the things I needed to do in order to have a great relationship with him: I could take on more responsibility for the project we were working on. I could be more proactive in setting deadlines. And it was rewarding to switch from anger to love. That's what this chapter is about because

> *anger is one of the most disabling emotions, particularly in communicating with other people. It stops clear thinking, kills happiness, and brings distress to both the mind and body. Being angry has little value in either the workplace or at home, and yet we do it constantly.*

In this chapter you will look closely at why and how you get angry. It will give you the experience of understanding that you can turn your anger off within seconds.

Anger Is Born Out of Fear

Anger is born out of fear and survival, leaving people freaked out, isolated, and upset. Everyone we have ever come into contact with has experienced anger at one time or another—some people manage it and others are managed by it. So what makes people manage their anger in a relationship? If we can manage anger in our own lives, in our personal relationships, we can manage anger with people at work—with coworkers and with customers. Anger is managed when we live in our human brain and realize that we can make a choice to fuel the anger or to fuel the love.

In the dictionary, *anger* means having a strong feeling of displeasure or hostility. So why do we become hostile or have strong feelings of displeasure with another human being?

It begins in the animal brain. Remember, the animal brain is all about survival. When one person is operating from his animal brain and the other person says or does something that puts his survival at risk— the animal brain will attack! By putting his survival at risk we are talking about things to do with money, home, food, job, relationships. Almost everything, in fact, has something to do with survival from the animal brain perspective.

That's what happens between partners, friends, family, coworkers, and customers. That's why there are so many wars, troubles, and so much upset! It has to do with people operating from their animal brains and from their basic feelings of survival.

Now if one person is operating from his animal brain and the other is operating from her human brain, there is a possibility of talking things out. The human being will allow the human animal to vent. If both people are operating from their animal brains, however, it is just two animals fighting.

And it only gets worse! The human animal can access additional intelligence and has many tools to fight with, including words, past indiscretions, bullying, holding back, lying, stonewalling . . . and on and on. The human animal is much more dangerous than the ordinary animal!

Fortunately, the human being is more amazing and powerful than the human animal. Just look at the amazing things that human beings do. Take, for example, Christy Brown, one of 23 children born to an Irish bricklayer. Christy had cerebral palsy, was declared at a very early age to be mentally defective, and it was said that nothing could be done for him. His mother, however, didn't believe this and said, "It is his body that is shattered, not his mind, I'm sure of it."

Christy's condition meant he couldn't control his speech or movement, except for his left foot. You may have heard his story, or seen the movie. One day while his sister was playing with some chalk and a blackboard, Christy picked up a piece of chalk with his left foot and made some marks with it. From that point on his mother taught him the alphabet, and after a slow and frustrating process, he gradually began to write, and developed a talent for painting using his left foot. At the age of 12 he won a *Sunday Independent* children's painting competition, and as he grew older wrote his autobiography, *My Left Foot*, four other novels, and a collection of poetry. Is that not a most amazing triumph of a human being?

Waking Up

There are thousands of stories of human beings triumphing over adversity, and while they may not be quite as astounding as Christy's, they are just as life affirming, like this e-mail tells us:

I was just thinking that I need to put a Post-it on my forehead saying "WAKE UP!" and then I remembered Switch, and I am smiling. I am affirming my day and being amazing. I must be handling my interactions with other human beings from a great place, because I see a lot more smiles coming my way—my ex is even smiling at me and he isn't even human. Okay, okay, maybe he is occasionally. My relationship with my kids is so much better. More hugs, more patience, more real communication, more fun. I do remember that the power is available to me to make a difference. I believe that it's everywhere and infinitely available to everyone. That works better for me because I get territorial when I think I have something, "HEY! THAT'S MY POWER. GIVE IT BACK!" You know what I mean? I have no idea how I will connect with other human beings today—so that they will get it that I've got it—but I know it will happen.

Did you get the bit about the "ex"? Remember, the human animal doesn't have any humor. So you know if someone is joking—they are beginning to switch on their human brain! And the bit about power—it's so true—power is everywhere and infinitely available to everyone. The territorial way of thinking about power is just like a black hole: it sucks everything, including all the power, into it until there is nothing left.

Even the most powerful people have to work on overcoming their animal brain—especially when it sends them spiraling into depression. Like the former prime minister of Great Britain, Winston Churchill, one of the most influential figures of World War II. In one of his best remembered speeches he said, "Never, never, never, never, never give in." His determination to overcome obstacles was best illustrated by his constant battle with depression (something he called his "little black dog"), which he never let affect his outcome.

Sun Tzu's Three Tenets

You only have to look back at history to see how others have overcome the animal brain of war and conflict. Sun Tzu, the Chinese general who wrote the book *The Art of War*, lived around the same time as Alexander the Great. But instead of developing a strategy typical of that period's war-fighting generals, Sun Tzu looked at war by examining it in the context of balance and harmony. He expressed it as "the three main tenets of the Art of War":

1. Work with nature by harmony and balance, not brute force.

2. Use intelligence to outwit the enemy.

3. Win by bluff and avoid fighting altogether.

These are noble ideals that we can use in switching from our animal brains to our human brains. If we think of our animal brains as something living inside us that we have to fight, a predator waiting to eat us up or a parasite sucking off us, we will experience being at war with ourselves. So looking at Sun Tzu's first tenet, why not work from a place of harmony and balance with our animal brains instead? For example, if you don't get along with someone, rather than spending hours talking about how much you dislike her, how horrible she is, what she did or did not do to you—instead of trying to get people on your side—work with the idea of harmony and balance.

A first step would be to look for the good in that person and for the good in yourself. If you can't find any good in the person, begin small. Maybe she has a great smile, dresses well, or always has a clean desk. Just find something, anything, that your human brain can focus on. The point is to feed the positive energy instead of the negative.

We received this great e-mail from a guy named Mike, about the importance of life itself:

> . . . when I make one person smile in a day, then I feel like my day is complete. Life is WAY too short to not be happy . . . even just earlier this year I turned 35 and my dad said, "Wow, you are getting old, I can't believe you're this old now." And me being me, I said, "Dad, I don't look at it that way anymore . . . yes, I'm getting older, and I can't believe I've been alive for 35 years. Think of how many people don't get to live for 35 years . . . knowing that a person can just die at any minute on any day and I'm still here to tell you this . . . it's amazing!"

In one spiritual tradition we know about, after a person dies, family and friends gather around and repeat three times, "Remember all your good deeds. Remember all your good deeds. Remember all your good deeds." This is a way of directing the deceased toward the light instead of toward the darkness. This is something we should all do as often as necessary: remember the good deeds we have done in order to keep ourselves lighthearted and positive.

Take a moment now to record at least five of your good deeds:

1. _____

2. _____

3. _____

4. _____

5. _____

And if you're not one to write things down, just take a moment and remember at least five good deeds that you have already accomplished in your life. They don't have to be huge things; they can be as simple as helping someone cross the road, cut the grass, or work out a math problem.

If you have serious anger problems, there are lots of anger management workshops to go to . . . and if you're an ordinary human being with the usual amount of anger that we all have, you can most likely manage it by switching, like this person told us:

> I have indeed been smiling more, and a positive attitude does get the best of me these days, even at home. I have been a negative person for many years. You have made me realize how to shake the bad attitude off my plate. I feel better about myself

with the exception of a few pounds I would like to take off, but that's everyone I think. Life is good. My family is healthy, beautiful, and loving. I really should not complain!

With lots of luck, Mary

Did you notice the animal brain and the human brain working together in Mary's e-mail? She's working on smiling more and shaking off her bad attitude, and then the animal brain comes in and says, "With the exception of a few pounds." You see, the animal brain does not want Mary to be completely happy. Her animal brain has the point of view that everyone wants to take off a few pounds, so it's okay to feel bad about it. That's the animal pack syndrome at work: we'll all go down the tubes together and then it won't be so bad—at least I won't be on my own.

And then, at the end of her e-mail, Mary says, "I really should not complain!" Is that the animal brain or the human brain, do you think? That's right, the animal brain. "I really should not complain—but I will." So what does Mary need to do? Affirm her day every morning by repeating what she said herself and what she knows is true: "Life is good. My family is healthy, beautiful, and loving."

Here's what one person wrote us after a Switch seminar:

Sometimes I forget about the daily affirmations first thing—so, many times it's in the car, talking to myself. Other drivers just keep their distance—LOL, laughing out loud. I know I can make a difference, and I think I have known this for a long time. My mother always told us, "You have to live with who you are, what you do, and the choices you make." Somewhere between when I first heard her say that and now, I really listened and understood.

Harmony and Balance

That first tenet of Sun Tzu—about working with nature, harmony, and balance, instead of brute force—is so helpful in switching from your animal to your human brain, because if you use brute force with your animal brain, it will rebel even more. So, for example, if you are more overweight than you care to be, the first step is to think kindly about your body. Have compassionate thoughts about your heart and how amazing it is to carry your extra pounds around. Instead of going on a brute force diet, be wise in your eating.

I know a guy who had a starring role in a production of *Joseph's Coat of Many Colors*. His costume was a toga, and there were times on stage when he barely wore anything. His partner said to him a couple of months before the show was due to begin, "Do you realize you're going to be showing your body to thousands of people very soon?" It had the effect of a sudden wake-up call.

"Ohmigod!" he said, and from that moment on he ate half of what he normally ate. He ordered his normal food, ate exactly the same things he had before . . . only half the amount! And that brings us to Sun Tzu's second tenet: Use intelligence to outwit the enemy.

Outwit the Animal Brain

Earlier we discussed not thinking of the animal brain as an enemy. We'll alter that here and say, in line with Sun Tzu's tenet, "use intelligence to outwit the animal brain." Like this person did who wrote us:

> I am continuing with the daily affirmations. I am also adding more every day that I need to affirm myself to. I cannot tell you the difference your seminar has made in both my personal and professional life. I will continue to live your lessons until I die.

Wow, isn't that amazing? There are so many stories of people using intelligence to overcome the most debilitating events of life. Like Professor Stephen Hawking, born in 1942, author of the book A *Brief History of Time*, who became a leading physicist and cosmologist. Typical of great minds, he overcame tremendous adversity to make his mark in our world. Although physically fit and athletic as a student, he suffered from a debilitating form of motor neuron disease that later confined him to a wheelchair and limits his communication to a computer-linked voice. Yet not only is he prolific in his academic and speaking activities, Hawking was awarded the Brain of the Year title in 1992, and as *Time* magazine stated, his mind continues "to soar ever more brilliantly across the vastness of space and time to unlock the secrets of the universe."

So use your intelligence when switching from your animal brain to your human brain. Don't become enemies with it. Instead you can silently say, "Thank you. I understand you're worried about my survival, and I'm fine. I am not being threatened; you can go rest a while, and I will operate from my human brain and see the funny side of this."

Have you ever been in the middle of an argument and suddenly seen the humorous side of it?

Maybe someone comes to the door and you have a truce and pretend to love each other until he has gone . . . and you want to laugh . . . the giggle is just on the edge of coming out, and then your animal brain says, "No! This is not funny. Remember what he just said (or did) to you? This is no time to laugh! This is serious."

Try it out the next time it happens—give in to the laughter. Use the smile. Find the humor. And you have to use your intelligence with it—because if the other person is in his animal brain, he will most likely take offense at you finding it funny. So be aware of that and give him a reason to find the funny side too.

Now, with customers, you definitely cannot start laughing or even smiling when they are in their animal brain and angry. You have to be in your human brain and in control of the situation. If the other person is angry, you know he's in his animal brain and coming from fear and survival, and you just have to let him vent. Defending, discussing, denying, or explaining will only get him to be more animalistic. So let him vent it out, and when he's calm, you can find the solution together and possibly a little, tiny bit of humor! This brings us to Sun Tzu's third tent: "Win by bluff and avoid fighting altogether."

Bluff and Avoidance

When a person is angry, she's operating from an animal brain that is not only out of control, but full of fear, and she can be as dangerous as a cornered animal. Obviously, there are levels of anger, but if the anger is chronic—if, for instance, something sets you off every day—then you need to use the bluff and avoidance tactic. Basically you bluff your animal brain into submission by pretending that everything is okay and there's nothing to fear. And if you can't think of even one good thing in your life to bluff your animal brain about—be thankful for just being alive. Like this person who wrote:

> When stepping out of bed in the morning, I thank God for another day and live it up to the fullest of my potential and enjoy everyone I meet. We are all so unique, and I can't help but marvel at what we are capable of accomplishing each day and throughout our lifetimes. When we interact with one another, what a wondrous force we can be in accomplishing anything.

Because the animal brain operates from fear and survival, it views everything and everyone as a potential threat. Your job is to operate from the human brain, which views everything and everyone as potentially safe and secure. People, including customers, coworkers, friends, and family, are not threatening when you operate from your human brain.

If you're so used to operating from your animal brain that you don't even know that you're fearful and living in survival mode, the bluff and avoidance technique is just what the doctor ordered. Here are the keys:

1. The first key is realization: "Wow, I do seem to be in a lot of arguments!" or "Wow, I spend a lot of time being angry!" or "I hate a lot of people in my life."

2. The second key is to want to avoid that kind of behavior.

3. The third key is bluffing it by having a human brain thought, something simple, like being thankful just to be alive.

Notice that you're not going to battle it, bury it, or deny it. Instead, you realize it's there and you simply want to avoid it for the moment. You can pick it back up tomorrow or next week or next year. For now, however, you simply want to avoid it. That way you're not at war with your animal brain; you are simply letting it rest in the corner. And like any animal that gets rest, it calms down. It becomes manageable, it becomes docile, it sleeps!

The way to avoid operating from your animal brain by avoidance is to use the bluff idea, to mislead or deceive it. Yes, it sounds a bit like an animal brain kind of tactic, doesn't it? And in a way it is—except that the animal brain is in fact misleading and deceiving you into being angry when there is often nothing to be angry about. It's just a habit. One day your animal brain decided it didn't like something or someone, and it just kept reinforcing that until it became a habit. Well, habits can be undone—and you can do it by bluffing.

Brain switchers will help you to bluff your animal brain into going from a red-alert, angry, survival mode to a green, cool, safe, secure mode, allowing you to operate fully from your human brain. We list these brain switchers below. Use them just for one day and notice the difference. At first it may feel that you are deceiving yourself—soon, however, it will become as much of a habit to operate from your human brain as it did to operate from your animal brain, when you were angry and upset. Like this person told us after a Switch seminar:

> This week has been great. The little changes are making a difference. Not only here at work, but at home where it counts the most.

BRAIN SWITCHERS TO HELP YOU BLUFF

As soon as you feel your animal brain igniting anger, avoid it with the following bluffs:

I am loved and taken care of.

I believe I have deep joy within me.

I am safe right now.

I rejoice in new possibilities.

I love and accept myself and others.

My energy is being uplifted in every moment.

I turn away from anger and embrace love in my life.

I have everything I want in my life and I want joy and peace.

I have the power to embrace a new way of being.

When I change my point of view to love—everything around me changes too.

When I see the miracle of life all around me, I realize I am a miracle too.

I have the power to operate from love and acceptance.

BRAIN SWITCHERS TO HELP YOU BLUFF (CONT.)

I am powerful beyond measure and I powerfully choose to love.

I am the source of my life and I create peace and harmony.

Two Steps to Take

Step 1. Take a moment now to write down one main thing that keeps you operating from your animal brain: _____

_____

Step 2. Now write down one main thing that will bluff the animal brain into operating from your human brain: _____

_____

You can use Step 2 as an affirmation to repeat in the morning or throughout the day to remind yourself to operate from the human brain instead of the animal brain. And if you are still having difficulties with this exercise, consider Helen Keller: what hope do you give a child who becomes blind and deaf before she is two years old and quite literally has the world shut out. Incredibly, through the persistence and love of her teacher, Anne Sullivan, Helen learned to read Braille and write using a special typewriter. Blessed with determination and courage to go beyond the limiting nature of her condition, she reached out and touched the world with her mind.

This is no different from what you are intending to do. Anger is no different than being blind and deaf! It stops you from seeing and hearing anything to do with love, acceptance, peace, and understanding. Anger is the animal brain operating from fear and survival. And just like any animal that feels trapped, it will do and say anything to get free . . . fight or flight.

It does take determination and courage to change your point of view from anger to peace, from fear to love, from survival to safe. And you can use the courage and determination of others to help you. As a baby Helen communicated through hysterical laughter and violent tantrums because she was scared to death. When someone began teaching her how to communicate, she eventually changed her whole life, graduating from college with honors and dedicating her life to raising money for the handicapped through her writing and lecturing. What amazing things will you do once you have tamed your animal brain into realizing it is safe?

Chapter Three

UNDERSTANDING HOW AMAZING YOU ARE AND THE POWER YOU HAVE

If I had my child to raise all over again, I'd finger paint more, and point the finger less. I'd do less correcting and more connecting. I'd take my eyes off my watch and watch with my eyes. I would care to know less and know to care more. I'd take more hikes and fly more kites. I'd stop playing serious, and seriously play. I'd run through more fields and gaze at more stars. I'd do more hugging and less tugging. I would be firm less often and affirm much more.

—Diane Looman
Full Esteem Ahead

Raising Yourself

Your customers expect you to know your job. What they are looking for is "what they want" above and beyond you just knowing the facts. They want a friendly, positive, confident, and solutions-oriented person to help them with whatever issue they have. If you've ever watched two- and three-year-olds playing, you'll understand that they have no concept of anything but being totally happy. They have unlimied energy and an amazing ability to look at everything with wide-open minds and huge eyes. Unfortunately, most of us have forgotten how much energy we have at our disposal and how amazing we are as individuals.

This chapter will rekindle, refocus, and enlighten you so that you become amazing every day. Not only will you realize the benefit, so will your customers (both internally and externally).

The one person it is most important to raise is you. You cannot raise other people, whether they are children, employees, customers, coworkers, spouses, family, or friends, until you begin to raise yourself. And how do you do that? You affirm your day! You begin to realize how amazing and powerful you are.

Affirming Your Day

Affirming your day is how you create a healthy environment for yourself. It is like the Broken Window theory, the brainchild of James Q. Wilson and George Kelling, who argued that crime is the inevitable result of disorder. If a window is broken and left unrepaired, people walk past feeling that no one cares and no one is in charge. Soon more windows get broken and a sense of decay and anarchy spreads throughout the neighborhood. This is accompanied with a feeling that anything goes, and soon the whole place is filled with crime and disease. It is the same with the animal brain.

If a person operates from their animal brain and is in fear and survival mode, he automatically creates an environment inside his mind that is like the Broken Window theory. Swearing becomes habitual, as does anger, depression, and worry. Soon the person is mixing with other people who have the same kind of habits, and thus the inner world creates the outer world, which in turn exacerbates the animal brain behavior among that group.

Affirming your day is the equivalent of putting your human brain in charge and your animal brain under orders—just like you have to train any animal.

The Good Samaritan

An interesting study was done at Princeton University by psychologists John Darley and Daniel Batson. It was related to the Good Samaritan story from the New Testament Gospel of Luke. Basically, they had seminarians prepare a short talk on a given biblical theme and then walk to a nearby building to present it. On their way, each seminarian ran across a man slumped in an alley, head down, eyes closed, coughing and groaning, and in obvious trouble. Some of the seminarians were told they were late and needed to quickly get to the building, while others were told to take their time. Of the group that were late, only 10 percent stopped to help the man. Of the group that had time to spare, 65 percent stopped.

Many speculations are made of studies like this—in the Switch theory it simply means that you have to switch on your human brain in order to be helpful. If someone is in trouble and you are operating from your human brain, you will stop and help and miraculous things happen. For example, what a great way for any of the seminarians to start their talk: "On the way over here I came across a man in the alley . . ." People are much more apt to listen to real-life experiences than a theoretical and dry dissertation.

When someone is in trouble and you are operating from your animal brain—like the seminarians who were fearful of being late—you will not even notice the person in trouble, and then a wonderful opportunity to be of help passes you by.

Recently, on a business trip to Brazil, I got to make two different choices because I live in the human brain. The first happened when I was flying to Brazil in the economy class of a 767 plane. There were three seats in the middle, and though I couldn't upgrade to business class, I was on the aisle of the first row of economy, with the extra leg room. I got on board and was putting my bags in the overhead compartment. It was a very full flight, and a lady in the middle seat was talking to a gentleman in the middle seat behind her. They were obviously together, and he said to me in broken English—because he was Brazilian—"Would you mind swapping seats with me so I could be with my wife?" My immediate reaction was No! I was on the aisle at the bulkhead with lots of room, and being over six feet tall that's important. He was asking me to go in the middle seat next to two other men for the whole 11-hour flight! My animal brain said, "Survive at any cost, this is not good."

Then I switched into my human brain and said to the man, "Yes, absolutely. Why don't you come and sit here." Of course I was inundated with praise and thank yous from his wife and from him because that allowed them to be together for the whole 11-hour flight. More important, I could be with myself and absorb a great sense of well-being for the entire 11 hours. I was thanked copiously again at the end of the flight, and as we were going through security I was again thanked by this couple. And I felt wonderful. After I swapped seats, the guy on my right turned to me and said, "Well done!" Of course, he could have swapped seats with the wife in the middle. Each of the surrounding passengers could have done something, but none of them did, and that's okay too. I got to make this choice, and although it was physically uncomfortable, I felt great.

The second choice happened because I'm always looking for the most efficient way to get things done. In the human brain, I am accepting of everything around me, and I can still be proactive and create the results I want. We don't have to just go along with the rest, like the herd. So coming back from Brazil, there were two ticket lines at the airport. Most people were standing in the longest line; and at first I thought if everyone is standing here, this must be the right line. Then I saw a much shorter line and thought, "Why am I standing here?" So I got into the shorter line. When I got to the front I realized it was only for business and first class. I still had my business-class card, but it had just expired, and I pointed this out to the ticketing agents. The agents and security people not only said, "That's fine sir," but because of my openness and honesty took me to the head of the economy-class line, and I got through the whole process in less than 12 minutes.

I find that when I operate from my human brain, with openness and honesty, people do even more, and every door is opened. Operating from your human brain creates a life of love in which you become a powerful leader.

What follows are 10 characteristics that let you know if you are in your human brain.

10 Characteristics of the Human Brain

1. **Love** is the ability to see the very best in people. Look at yourself and others with love and recognize you are all the same. As human beings we all want to love and be loved.

2. **Accept** and believe that goodness will prevail. Accept yourself the way you are and the way you are not and you will live a powerful life. When you accept other people as they are and as they are not, your life will blossom in ways you cannot even begin to imagine.

3. **Create** and know that you are living an amazing life. You only have to look around and see the amazing things that we human beings create. If you want to create laughter in your life, begin by laughing at yourself and be willing for others to laugh with you, at you, and alongside you.

4. **Peace** is the powerful antidote to war. It happens every time a person puts down the sword, takes off the shield, and decides to be a human being. It happens when you stop in the middle of a battle or an argument and take a deep healing breath to connect with the universal breath. U*ni-verse*—one song. And the wonderful thing is, there is always someone singing!

5. **Bliss** is that moment when you stop and breathe in all of nature's glory. It happens when you acknowledge a blue sky, a green tree, a red rose, a bird in flight, a sunbeam, or a blade of grass. Connect with nature for just a moment and experience your place in the miracle of life.

6. **Humor** is the joy of being. Seeing the funny side of things will keep you young at heart and brighten your life. Notice what makes you laugh and follow the directions: *one good dose of humor three times daily.*

7. **Joy** fills your heart with oxygen and keeps your mind focused on goodness. Joy often comes from simple things that you experience, like watching the sunset, getting a letter of acceptance, or being told you did a great job.

8. **Forgive** yourself and forgive others. One of the goals of life is to die forgiven and forgiving of everyone in your life!

9. **Understand** you are a human being and so is everyone else. Even the most macabre human animals have a human brain—endeavor to understand that and you will be an evolving human being.

10. **Passion** is the fire that creates amazing things. It burns with a light that gives life to everything you want to create. Keep it burning by loving what you do and doing what you love.

FORGIVENESS EXERCISE

Here's a powerful exercise on forgiveness. The person or people you forgive do not have to be present for you to do it.

1. Close your eyes.

2. Imagine the person you want to forgive in front of you. Visualize looking into his eyes and repeat these words to him: "Please forgive me for everything that I have knowing-

---

FORGIVENESS EXERCISE (CONT.)

ly or unknowingly done to hurt you. I forgive you for everything that you have knowingly or unknowingly done to hurt me."

3. When you are complete, you may feel a sudden rush of warmth, love, or even sadness. Just allow it to be. Know that you have energetically cleared a great space by your willingness to forgive and be forgiven!

Energy

We were talking about this thing called energy just the other day. About how it's so easy to see and experience the world from a material perspective because you can see the chair you sit on, the bed you sleep in, the car you drive, the clothes you wear, and so on. These are all real and solid objects that have color, shape, size, weight, and texture to them. Yet, if you were to view all these material objects through a powerful microscope, you would see more space than solid material. And in the space you would see quarks and leptons, the building blocks upon which matter is made.

Physicists have uniquely named these quarks down, charm, strange, top, and bottom. And we're told that if two physicists with different expectations complete the same experiment on a quark, their outlook will affect the result. So if everything is shaped by our outlook, by the way we look at things, then we can decide what results we want to create and proceed to look at things from a result-oriented perspective instead of just being a victim to whatever comes along—as if you have no part in shaping the outcome of your life.

So what results do you want to create? If you always create difficult customer service situations—or difficult personal relationships—you need to look at the way you are viewing the situation. Are you expecting it to be difficult? Because if so, then guess what you are creating? That's right, a difficult relationship.

Here is an exercise for you to do that will turn things around. It may take you a day, a week, or a month to complete. It doesn't matter, because time also is something we make up. If you are chronically late, does that mean you have less time than someone who is chronically early? No! You just view time differently. Being on time is easy when you look at it from an "I create the results I want" perspective. If you are meeting someone at noon, work backward from that time: it takes 10 minutes to drive, 5 minutes to stop for gas, 5 minutes to park, and I want to arrive 5 minutes early. I need to leave at 11:35!

THOUGHTS, ACTIONS, AND RESULTS EXERCISE

You can return to this exercise at a later date to record your results. Also, be open-minded and nonjudgmental about yourself—in other words, don't have any preconceived expectations.

1. In the space below, please write down a result that you would like to happen in your life. It could be with a relationship, money, career, or something else. Just one other note: make it something about yourself—this is not about changing someone else, this is about a result for you. Also, be as brief as possible in describing the result you want: _____

2. Next, think of one main action that will help you achieve your result. For example, the result you want could be to have *peace-*

THOUGHTS, ACTIONS, AND RESULTS EXERCISE (CONT.)

ful communications with your customers. The main action would be to *not take anything a customer says or does personally.* In the space below, write down the main action you need to take in order to achieve the result you want. Action I will take: _____

_____

3. Based on the above action, write down an affirmation that you are willing to say every morning. Using our example, the affirmation could be, "Every customer interaction will be an opportunity to not take things personally": _____

4. This is the step that you will return to when you have achieved the results you want. In the space below write two dates: The first is today's date. The second is the date upon which you achieved your result!

Today's date: _____

Date I achieved my result: _____

Chapter Four

FROM AVERAGE TO OUTSTANDING CUSTOMER SERVICE

We are what we repeatedly do. Excellence, then, is not an act, it is a habit.

—Aristotle

Being Outstanding

In this chapter we will look at how we have fallen into the trap of staying in our comfort zones. We have become habitual in the way we do our jobs, the way we live our lives, and the relationships that we have created. In other words, we have become comfortable. To be outstanding, you must step outside your comfort zone so that you stand ready to be amazing.

Recently I was talking with a friend, Angela, about the difficulty of switching. She said:

> I don't know if it's always possible to switch. Earlier this year I had a problem in my throat and had to have a biopsy. For a whole week I was really worried about whether I had cancer of the throat! I

thought about, what if I died? What would my family do without me? It was one of the worst weeks of my life. I don't think I could have switched—or even if I should have switched.

Angela went on to say that while Switch is okay in everyday life, when there is a life and death situation like the one she went through, it is impossible to switch.

Well, it may be for a while, and yet ultimately there is still a choice. How do I want to be in this situation? If you ever read the book *Tuesdays with Morrie*, you know that he made the choice to go through his illness with love. He celebrated his life up to the very end—and died in the midst of love. He made the choice to be in his human brain.

Switch Is Being Truthful

Switch is not about putting on a brave act as much as it is about being truthful. When I went through my own cancer scare over 15 years ago, I became very afraid of dying. I cried and got depressed, and then I realized I had a choice: did I want to make my children afraid of dying, or did I want to be amazing and brave and let them know that we all have to die eventually?

It's okay to cry and wail and moan about our life. The question is this: "How long do I want to be in that space?" There would appear to be a payoff to being afraid. When I lie in bed depressed and full of fear, I don't have to do anything! And if I am ill, I can ask for a glass of water to be brought to me—which I did, frequently!

And then I decided, "Enough is enough!" I realized it would be better to think about how amazing my life is and how thankful I am for everything in it. I started listing all the things I was thankful for: all the people who care for me; the doctors who are working to make me well again; the medicines that help take away the pain; the people who have found new ways of healing.

Afterward, I began to feel lighter, and I think that's what helped me heal. I took the burden of disease and turned it into a triumph of life. Switch is about aligning yourself with one voice—the voice that comes from universal energy—a higher power. It is about aligning yourself with love instead of fear.

In the animal brain, it is impossible to hear the voice of a higher power. There is so much fear and survival going on that it becomes like static. The receiver simply does not work. In the human brain there is a clear channel. Love is light. Fear is dark. In the darkness it is hard to think about anything except the dark, which is why it is sometimes difficult to switch. And yet when you think about it, all you have to do is switch on the light.

Yesterday, our daughter was in the office, and a woman who works here said, "It is so wonderful to see the way you are with each other. You have fun and you are playful. I could never be that way with my parents. I was too scared of them. If I said anything, they always made me wrong." I went on to tell her that we also have our moments when we get frustrated with each other. When we get into the parent-child routine of not wanting to see the other's point of view, the only difference is that we know to switch so it doesn't last long. Because what is the point of being right and all alone, like this person who wrote us realized:

> I am going through a very tough time in my life, and the timing of your e-mail was incredible. I just realized I was operating in the wrong brain. Unhealthy thoughts were consuming my mind making it difficult to work, sleep, and operate as the healthy single parent that I am. A simple reminder such as this will change the way my life has been going the last two weeks, and I am going

> to start being a blessing to my family and cowork-
> ers. I just realized how many people love us and
> have made a difference in our lives. I reminded
> myself of a saying that goes, "The way you see your
> life shapes your life." I am an amazing person and
> so is my daughter, and I am going to give her a
> hug and tell her so after school. We both are going
> to do amazing things and make the difference in
> many lives down the road of life.

As the writer of this e-mail reminds us, "The way you see your life shapes your life!" It's that simple and that difficult. Early on in our lives we were given the mechanical animal brain program of seeing life from fear and from survival. As a result, when a customer walks in or calls on the phone, they are seen and heard from the viewpoint of fear and survival: "Here comes another one wanting more than I can give. Here comes another one who is angry and frustrated. Here comes another one who is going to make my life miserable. Here comes another one with problems I can't solve."

From the point of view of the animal brain, the customer is doomed before they even speak—they have ceased to be a human being, they're just a number, like you sometimes see at the deli counter:

"Number 62!" From the perspective of the mechanical animal brain program, it doesn't matter how many customer service books you read or workshops you go to, the customer is just a big nuisance.

It's not that the animal brain is the "wrong brain." Once you start thinking like that, you will come up against resistance and create a lot of problems for yourself. The animal brain is there for your survival, to make sure you do not put your hand in boiling water, throw yourself off the bridge, or walk down dark alleys in the middle of the night without some kind of protection. Your animal brain is there to protect you. It's as simple as that. The problem is, because the animal brain comes from fear and survival, it is very simple—one dimensional—blind to all the amazing things that the human brain can see.

From the human brain, which operates from love, the customer is a human being who needs our support and assistance. When customers walk in or call on the phone, the human brain sees them as an opportunity to be amazing—kind of like a Sherlock Holmes—and looks for clues about how to solve things. The human brain is curious and wants to find out more about the situation so it can help find a solution. So it can help resolve something for another human being.

Here's an e-mail we received recently:

Hi, *how are you? I took your seminar three years ago. It was a superior class and I learned a lot. I am having problems in myself. My brain is not working right. I am having an animal brain now. As an example, I cannot do what I determined to do. I cannot finish what I started. There is something in my mind not working. Can you please help me?*

Thanks, Claire

Here's what we e-mailed back:

Dear Claire,

Thanks for responding to my e-mail and of course I would love to help you. You are doing really well, because all change begins with a realization that you want to do something differently. You want to operate from your human brain instead of from your animal brain. From my experience, the best way to do what you say you are going to do, and to finish what you start, is to affirm your day every morning. Look in the mirror, and say, "Today I will operate from my human brain. I will finish what I start and do what I say I am going to do." Remember you have the choice to live the life you want to live. That is what is so wonderful about being a human being—it is your choice.

Everything Is a Choice

Everything you do in your life begins with a choice, and it begins from the moment you wake up in the morning. It begins with your very first thought. "Do I want to wake up happy or not happy? Do I want to leap out of bed alive and enthusiastic to start another wonderful day, or do I want to crawl out of bed feeling dead and asleep?" And then it continues—your choice, your thought. "Do I want to make the bed so I come back tonight and the bed looks inviting, or do I not want to make the bed so that I come back tonight and it still looks rumpled and unkempt?"

And it follows you into the bathroom: "Do I want to sing in the shower and be full of joy, or do I want to stumble into the shower and be dull." And when you look in the mirror to brush your teeth and your hair, shave or put makeup on, your choice continues: "Do I see myself as a beautiful human being, full of untapped potential, or do I see myself as ugly and hopeless?"

Your choice of how you live your life continues like this all day long: "Do I want to eat healthy food and feel energized by the fuel I have just put into my body, or do I want to eat unhealthy food and feel lethargic and sleepy?"

And with customers your choice is always there—with every interaction: "Do I want to be helpful and find solutions that give me a sense of accomplishment, or do I want to be unhelpful and feel frustrated and have to deal with angry people and their problems?"

Then when you get home at night the choice continues. Do you want to view your personal life to be full of problems, no money, no relationship, difficult people, and hard times? Or do you want to view your personal life as being full of opportunities to create a different point of view?

How You See Shapes Your Life

If you see your life as having no money, then you create having no money. If you see your life as having no relationship, then you create having no relationship. If you see your life surrounded by difficult people, then you create having difficult people in your life. The way you see your life shapes your life. It seems too simple, doesn't it? How can it be?

Claire, who e-mailed us that "I cannot do what I determined to do. I cannot finish what I started," is creating exactly that because that is what she is telling herself. If you tell yourself that you are no good at math, what do you create? That you are no good at math! This is something I used to tell myself, and it came from a program I was given over 40 years ago by a math teacher who told me, "You are no good at math!"

Now imagine a young student who is told by an older teacher, "You are no good at math." Is that young student going to think, "Yes I am!" or, "Oh no. I'm no good at math!" After I was given this program, for years I thought I was no good at math, until I recently had the realization that I am in fact extremely good at math. I just never saw myself that way, and then one day someone in the office said, "I've got to send out 55 manuals at $150 each, how much is that?"

Within a couple of seconds I worked it out in my head and responded, "It's $8,250!" Then I realized I do that a lot and don't even know how I do it. I just have an ability to visualize numbers and come up with the answer.

This is how we get our animal program. We buy into the fear. "Oh no—I'm no good at this; I'm no good at that." And then it becomes real to us. Except it is not real; it is just someone else operating out of their animal brain who is an authority and telling us what we should believe.

Not so long ago people believed the Earth was flat. It sounds ridiculous now because we go into space and take photographs of our planet and we can see that it is not flat, and yet that's what people believed. That if they went too far across the ocean in their wooden ships with billowing sails, they would eventually come to the end of the Earth and literally "drop off"! And these were intelligent people back then. They knew a lot of things. They knew how to make tools to build boats, houses, wheels, complicated armor, castles with moats and drawbridges. They knew how to read, write, and farm the land to grow crops. Yet they believed the Earth was flat and lived in fear of traveling too far lest they fall off the edge!

If they believed something that seems so ludicrous to us now, is there a possibility that we too believe things that will seem ludicrous to our great-great-great-grandchildren? Of course—how can it be otherwise? Do you see? We're making it all up in our heads, because most of the time we're operating from beliefs that we believe are true.

If you believe one of your coworkers is depressing to be around and you dislike being around him, guess what you're creating? A depressing coworker. You have put him in the box, and that is where he will stay. For him to get out of the box and become a happy person in your eyes, you would have to be wrong! And the animal brain coming from fear and survival can never be wrong. So your poor coworker will never get out of the box you have put him in.

It's the same with everyone in your life. If you believe someone in your life is no good, you will put him in a box labeled NO GOOD and it will be very difficult for him to get out. You even stop looking for the good in him. Even if he does something good, from your animal brain perspective you will say, "He did good for a no-good kind of person."

We Create Our World

The world we create comes from the thoughts from which we create it. For example, what kind of a world do you think the sender of the following e-mail is building?

> Hi, just a quick note to say thanks for sending out these e-mails. In this crazy busy world we are building, there never seems to be enough time to do the things we really want to do; and things like your e-mail encouragements that remind us of our incredible powers are all too often overlooked. Please know they are very much appreciated.

It's wonderful to hear from clients who appreciate our motivational e-mails that remind them to operate from their human brain. At the same time it's impossible not to notice that the sender of this e-mail is building a busy world in which there is never enough time to do the things he really wants to do! If we do not do the things we want to do now, when will we do them? Part of being great at providing service is to provide service to ourselves. We have to nourish the customer inside of us—the human being who wants to achieve amazing things and make a difference in people's lives. Human beings love to create wonderful things, healthy environments in which people can live without fear. Human beings want to help people and support and assist them in becoming human beings themselves.

If you don't like the environment you're in—if it's too busy for you—then you have a choice. You always have a choice when you are operating from your human brain. You can choose to enjoy it, or choose to leave it. Those are the only two choices you have from the human brain. From the animal brain you simply don't like it and will put up with it even if it is silently killing you, because from the animal brain perspective you have no choice. The animal brain is all about survival, and to survive it will do anything—even stay in a job or a relationship that is slowly killing it. A person operating from their animal brain who does not like their job, for example, will think they are providing good customer service. They will say the right words and then wonder why the customer responds in an angry way. And, as determined by a University of Pennsylvania study, that is because words are only 7 percent of how we communicate thoughts and ideas. The tone of voice is 38 percent, and body language is 55 percent.

A person can say "I love you!" so it comes across as "I hate you!" If a customer is dealing with a person who is operating from his animal brain, the only chance of getting a problem resolved is for the customer to operate from her human brain. Then she can at least stop the customer service provider from creating an even worse problem, like losing the paperwork or writing down a wrong delivery date.

Remember, when people operate from their animal brains, it only creates a no-win scenario—it is impossible to do anything else. Like this e-mail we received that shows an animal brain in action. Here's what the writer said about her son's father:

> . . . his dad has been extremely discouraging to him, refusing to attend his graduation ceremonies and discouraging him from going to college. Not to worry, he will be attending university in the fall . . .

Why would a father operating from his human brain refuse to attend his son's graduation ceremony and discourage him from going to college? Is there something else going on here? Is it about money? I don't know. I do know that the only person who really suffers is the son. Yes, he's going to college, and yet how much better would it be if he went with both parents approval.

And the son has a choice too. He can choose to wake up in the morning happy or unhappy. I know it sounds too simple . . . and it is. Personal power comes from all the choices that you make in your day. It does not come from going to a workshop, getting a lot of wonderful information about how to be enlightened, and then next morning waking up feeling depressed and unhappy about your life and making the choice to be unhappy for the rest of the day.

Personal Power

Personal power comes from doing the things you don't want to do. A depressed person does not want to make the choice to be happy. Like the woman I met recently who has been married for 40 years and says that she's been depressed and unhappy for most of her life. She then went on to explain that it's in her genes. Her mother was depressed and her sisters are depressed.

Now, I have personal knowledge of family genes being something of a struggle to overcome. My father was an angry man, and my mother got depressed . . . so I know that I have that program within me, and I also know that I have a choice. I can choose to go with my family program or I can *switch* to my human brain and go with a larger family program and access the genes of ancestors who were happy and fully operating from their human brains. There had to be someone in the mix like that.

Anyway, this woman said of her husband, "My husband is very supportive of me. He loves to do yoga. He would like me to do it too, only I don't like it . . . " So what does "my husband is very supportive of me" actually mean? I don't know because I did not get a chance to ask her. But later I wondered if it means that he takes her coffee in bed because she is too unhappy to get up in the morning. Does it mean that he says, "Don't worry, dear, you can be sad and unhappy and I will still be happy around you." Does it mean, "I am going to be happy in spite of you and do my yoga and live a separate life?"

I have no idea. We can never know what goes on in people's lives. I do know that she has a choice. Small steps at first—wake up and make the choice to be happy. Get out of bed and make the choice to make the bed. Go in the shower and make the choice to sing. Look in the mirror and make the choice to see the beautiful you. Like this person who sent us an e-mail:

> Hi there. Yes I am doing great, I work for a won-
> derful company, my personal life is doing very well,
> I am getting married soon, so my mind is very
> busy with the preparations for that. I don't really

like at all what I do here and I work every single day to be better, to become a better person and a better professional so someone can see it and how proactive I am and then I can change my position pretty soon. And I do have to work on it, and everything in life takes time.

I am sure I am what I am just because of me, I am not going down, I am a very strong person who knows crying won't fix the problem. Most of the time I have been by myself and have had to learn how to take care of me. I know I have to think positive, so positive things will come to me—like this company, my coworkers, my bosses, and like you and your Super Service training. I think I was born to touch others with my way to be. So they can stop and think about it, and have the chance to change, and to me that's GREAT! Thank you for your training, it was just on time for many of us. And because of it there is a partner that has changed a lot—this person looks different to me with his actions. I am sure he began to change just after your training. And because of it THANK YOU. I hope to hear about you in the future. So you can touch us with your special messages!

All the best, Cynthia

Sweet, isn't it? Here is a person struggling and making the choice to be amazing in her life. She doesn't like her job too much and she is working on being great so she can get a different position. She talks about being "born to touch others with my way to be . . ." And the amazing thing is that we all are! You are touching people every day with your "way to be." The way that you wake up in the morning touches everyone close to you. If you have a spouse, you will help make his or her day great or not because, although it is your spouse's choice alone, it's wonderful when we support each other in operating from our human brain, instead of our animal brain.

When you walk into work, you touch people with your "way to be." Even if you don't say a word, people immediately know if you made the choice to be happy this morning or made the choice to be unhappy. Without saying a word, you are encouraging people to come up to you, smile, and say, "Good morning!" or stay away from you and give each other the look that says, "Ooops, she's in a bad mood again—better stay away!"

Then you wonder why no one comes over and talks to you. Why you feel so alone. Why you feel you have no friends and why no one loves you. Every human being wants the same thing—to love and be

loved. The human animal doesn't care about love—
it doesn't care if you are alone every night sad and
depressed. It doesn't care if you send out signals that
keep people away. All it cares about is your survival,
and to the animal brain, it's easier not having to deal
with people.

Problems Move Us Forward

The human brain operates from the understanding
that problems are okay. Helping customers handle
problems is part of the job. Problems move us forward; they are there to show that we are still alive. We
are not dead; our heart line is still going up and
down—we don't have a flat line yet!

And as we said earlier, your environment does
influence how you feel. Like the man I talked with who
recently changed jobs and is now working as an
inside salesperson in a large outbound call center
with 55 other men and women. He used to work in a
small, quiet office, and this new job is a great opportunity for him to be with other people. However, as
he told me, "People are crashing their phones down
and shouting *blank* you into the receiver!" And he lit-

erally shouted out the obscene word as he described it, saying, "A couple of guys almost broke out into a fight the other day!"

So I asked him, "Do you like it!"

"I *blankety blank* love it," he said. "It's like being in a *blankety blank* shark tank! Everyone is so competitive."

I had to laugh to myself later, because this same person used to comment if someone even spoke a mild swear word out loud. So the environment was certainly having its effect on him . . . and as he said, "he *blankety blank* loves it." His choice. His life. His job.

The important thing for you to consider is: do you love your life and your job? If not, you can do something to change it. Like Cynthia, whom we quoted earlier, says, "I don't really like at all what I do here and I work every single day to be better . . . so someone can see it and how proactive I am and then I can change my position pretty soon."

Your job—your life—your choice.

Chapter Five

HANDLING THE WORKLOAD

This is the true joy in life, the being used for a purpose recognized by yourself as a mighty one, the being thoroughly worn out before you are thrown on the scrap heap. The being a force of nature instead of a feverish little clod of ailments and grievances, complaining that the world will not devote itself to making you happy.

I am of the opinion that my life belongs to the whole community, and as long as I live it is a privilege to do for it what I can. I want to be thoroughly used up when I die, for the harder I work the more I live.

I rejoice in life for its own sake. Life is no brief candle to me. It is a sort of splendid torch, which I've got to hold up for the moment. I want to make it burn as brightly as possible before handing it on to future generations.

—George Bernard Shaw
Irish literary critic, playwright, and essayist (1856–1950)

How You Spend Your Time

People who are amazing and achieve a lot seem to have a lot of time to do lots of things. In this chapter we will look closely at how you spend your time on the job. Do you walk into work in the morning with several goals you'd like to achieve and end up achieving nothing and going home frustrated? Well, it stops now. We will look closely at the whole concept of time and getting caught up in the routine of the job and your life. By the end of the chapter you will be able to manage your time and feel a sense of accomplishment at the end of every day. And who benefits? *Everyone*!

When you operate from your animal brain, you live in fear—fear of losing your job, fear of losing your beloved, fear that something horrendous will happen to your children, fear of not having enough money to retire, fear of ending up unloved and unwanted . . . fear, fear, and more fear. There is an unlimited supply of things to be fearful about, and what happens to people who are fearful is that they end up bent and doubled over with all the fear the animal brain puts on their back.

Why does the animal brain want to constantly remind you of all the things you need to be afraid of? Because it is only interested in your survival. It is constantly on the lookout for things to go wrong, for things that go bump in the night, for disasters to overcome. When you operate from this fear, you go into overdrive. It's a bit like a frantic animal trying to escape from a trap. You may have heard stories about trapped animals and even human animals going to unbelievable lengths to set themselves free—like even biting through a limb! Yet, most of the time we are not in a desperate survival situation— we don't need to operate from that kind of fear.

When you operate from your human brain, time has a way of expanding. You will find time to sit down and read a book, watch a favorite TV show, do whatever it is that you love to do to replenish your batteries. And it's from the human brain, of course, that you remember that your life is about being an amazing human being.

Creating Miracles

An amazing friend of ours wanted a new deck on the back of her home. She heard of a builder who used good materials and could complete the deck in a timely manner. The only problem was the cost. He wanted $500 more than she could afford. He said he could do it in the next few days, and so she told him she would think about it.

The next day, she got a check from her mortgage company that would not only cover the cost of the deck, but also enable her to buy some furniture for it, and some trees for the yard. Excited, she called and told me about her good fortune. I asked her, "What do you think you did to manifest the money you needed?"

"I just kept being happy," she said. "I know the universe is abundant, and I kept focusing on that rather than getting upset about not having enough money for the deck."

Coaching Yourself

Many people who can't get something they want begin to feel frustrated and end up feeling bad. It's the same with handling your workload. If you're constantly being overworked, you need to do some practical inquiry into what is happening and what you can do about it.

Here are some questions you can ask yourself to gauge how you're handling your workload:

1. How do you feel about how you handle your workload? _____

   _____

2. What three things could you do differently to change your experience?

   a. _____
   b. _____
   c. _____

3. How will you incorporate these changes?

   a. _____
   b. _____
   c. _____

This kind of practical inquiry is a way of finding out what to do if you aren't handling your workload effectively. It is a way of coaching yourself. You always have the right answers within you . . . they just need to come out so you can hear them.

Chapter Six

E-MAIL IS INFORMATION, NOT COMMUNICATION

The following words are written on the tomb of an Anglican Bishop (AD 1100) in the crypts of Westminster Abbey:

> When I was young and free and my imagination had no limits, I dreamed of changing the world. As I grew older and wiser, I discovered the world would not change, so I shortened my sights somewhat and decided to change only my country.
>
> But it too, seemed immovable.
>
> As I grew into my twilight years, in one last desperate attempt, I settled for changing only my family, those closest to me, but alas, they would have none of it.
>
> And now as I lie on my deathbed, I suddenly realize:
>
> If I had only changed myself first, then by example I would have changed my family.
>
> From their inspiration and encouragement, I would then have been able to better my country, and who knows, I may have even changed the world.

E-mail Is an Amazing Tool

Whenever we facilitate a focus group about communication, e-mail always comes out as one of the top problems that need to be solved—so we need to look closely at how we are using e-mail and why is it such a problem. Used properly, e-mail is one of the most amazing tools of the twenty-first century; therefore, this chapter is devoted to giving you seven rules on how to make e-mail an amazing tool instead of an amazing gruel.

Remember, in business, e-mails are about giving information; they are not for communication. If you are having difficulties with an individual, e-mail is not the answer. If you are having problems with a project, e-mail is not the best way to handle it. If you have an important project that requires communication between departments and people, remember to connect with them physically, either by telephone or face-to-face. E-mail is fantastic for sending information or for sending motivational reminders like we do for the people who have participated in our workshops, but used improperly, it can isolate people and create havoc and chaos.

We know there are numerous programs out there that will teach you the proper use of e-mail. The problem is, even if you get the right tools, if you're in your animal brain, you'll either forget to use the tools or manipulate them in some way so that you *seem* to be using the tools, when in fact you are not.

Conversely, if you're in your human brain, you will use e-mail to effectively provide information in a clear, concise way, so that the receiver of the e-mail is updated with new information instead of being swamped with nonuseful stuff. So here are the rules of how to use e-mail from your human brain and get amazing results from your colleagues, family, and friends.

Rule 1: Tailor your e-mails to your audience. *"All that we are is a result of what we have thought."* Abraham Lincoln

Rule 2: Only send motivational e-mails if you are walking your talk. *"It is no use walking anywhere to preach unless our walking is our preaching."* St. Francis of Assisi

Rule 3: Before hitting Send, always reread your e-mail thinking: Is it wise, kind, or necessary? *"Every problem has in it the seed of its own solution, if you have no problems you don't have any seeds."* Dr. Norman Vincent Peale

Rule 4: Before you e-mail a problem for someone else to solve, first look at solving it yourself. *"Our doubts are traitors, and make us lose the good we oft might win by fearing to attempt."* William Shakespeare

Rule 5: Your e-mail may be forwarded and end up before many pairs of eyes—make sure what you are saying is something you don't mind the whole world reading! *"Judge each day not by the harvest you reap but by the seeds you plant."* Robert Louis Stevenson

Rule 6: Create your e-mails as messengers of opportunity. Ask yourself: What specific information do they need? What answers do I need back? When do I need to hear back? *"There is never any hurry on the creative plane, and there is no lack of opportunity."* Wallace D. Wattles

Rule 7: Your e-mails send a strong message about you. Did you bother with spell-check? Did you edit out the needless stuff? What does this e-mail say about you? *"We either make ourselves miserable, or we make ourselves strong, the amount of work is the same."* Carlos Castaneda

One of our clients asked us to participate in a focus group about how to write effective e-mails. First, everyone in the group had to read *The Elements of Style* by William Strunk, Jr. and E. B. White. Then everyone received five e-mails to edit. Because I write for a living, my e-mails always received the highest score and were put on their intranet as examples of how to write effective e-mails. To give you an idea of how to edit your e-mails, here's an example of an e-mail I received just the other day:

Hi *there,*

Do you remember a lady called Mary Bench? She ran the accounts department for our company and is a friend of Betty's. Mary now runs a small

training company that works with "Investment Analysis." This is a three-day workshop on solving questions either personal or company. Small, but starting to grow quite well. Mary is in your location next week and I hope you do not mind but I have given her your e-mail to contact you. If you have time it could be a great exchange of ideas, as she knows many people and your products could be joined in some way. (106 words)

Here's my edit:

Hi there,

Hope all is well! Remember Mary Bench, who ran accounts? She now runs a small and growing "Investment Analysis" training company. She's in your location next week. She knows many people, and your products could be joined in some way. Here's her e-mail—mary@Inva—if you have time to meet and exchange ideas. I told her you might be in touch. (63 words)

My edit incorporates a greeting and still uses almost half the words. It gets the message across, keeps my e-mail address private, and leaves me in charge of whether or not to contact Mary.

Short and to the Point

We have talked to some managers who literally have hundreds of e-mails in their in-box every day. It's just a courtesy to make yours as succinct as possible— short and to the point, and informative without being overwritten. If your e-mail has too many words before it gets to the content—it could very well be deleted.

A couple of final thoughts about e-mails: Many of the people who complain about too many e-mails are actually the ones sitting at their desks writing e-mails to coworkers who are sitting less than five feet away! Our recommendation is to get up, walk to the person, and ask the question—maybe they don't need the five-page report!

Finally, chain e-mails: If you are one of those people who send "good luck" e-mails that have to be forwarded to 10 other people for the luck to happen, maybe you should e-mail the people on your list and find out if they actually want to be a regular recipient of your good intentions. There is nothing worse than being extremely busy and having to make the decision to delete an e-mail along with a possible deletion of good luck!

So if you have read this chapter and feel the need to clean up your e-mails, think about this Turkish proverb: "No matter how far you have gone on the wrong road, turn back."

Chapter Seven

BECOME THE OBSERVER, NOT THE ABSORBER

If you woke up this morning with more health than illness, you are more blessed than the millions who will not survive the week. If you have never experienced the danger of battle, the loneliness of imprisonment, the agony of torture, or the pangs of starvation, you are ahead of 500 million people around the world. If you attend a church meeting without fear of harassment, arrest, torture, or death, you are more blessed than almost 3 billion people in the world. If you have food in the refrigerator, clothes on your back, a roof over your head, and a place to sleep, you are richer than 75 percent of this world. If you have money in the bank, in your wallet, and spare change in a dish someplace, you are among the top 8 percent of the world's wealthy. If your parents are still married and alive, you are very rare. If you hold up your head with a smile on your *face and are truly thankful, you are blessed because the majority can, but most do not. If you can read this message, you are more blessed than over 2 billion people in the world who cannot read anything at all.*

—Unknown

Observer Not Absorber

Have you noticed how easy it is to give other people advice? When they talk to you about problems they are having with their colleagues, their customers, or their spouses, it's easy for us to give advice because we are the observer not the absorber. Billions of dollars are wasted every year in the workplace trying to resolve conflicts between human beings. We have to become the observer of the uncomfortable situation that we come up against, not the absorber. As an absorber you will become emotional, take it personally, and come from fear that leads to anger and depression. When you observe yourself in the uncomfortable position, you see everything clearly and don't have to be at the mercy of anything or anyone again.

I heard a guru once say to his students, "I walked into the temple this morning and I saw a woman weeping in a chair. Everyone was walking around her and acting as if nothing was happening. This woman was in distress, yet nobody went up to her and asked to help her. When I told you to become the observer, I did not mean you should become indifferent to suffering!"

As a human being, it's difficult to watch any kind of suffering and not be affected. As a human animal, it's not difficult to watch suffering, because the animal brain doesn't even register suffering. People operating from their human brains have the choice to observe and take the right *action*. People operating from their animal brains have no choice except to absorb and *react*. See those two words? *Action*: the state or process of doing. *React*: to act in response to a prompt or influence. Action is about having the power to act. Reaction is being under the power of someone or something else.

Taking Action

When you take appropriate action, you are choosing to do something. You are in the power seat and you have all the control. You can take your time, you can schedule events, you can set goals, you can choose to do it great or even sloppily—the point is you are in charge.

When you react there is no choice involved; you are under the influence of a stimulus and you react with a knee-jerk response. You are like a puppet under the control of a puppeteer. If the puppeteer is angry, he is going to pull your strings in an angry way. If the puppeteer is sad, he will control you in a sad way. If you're with a customer, for example, and you are in your animal brain, you will react in response to her influence and be at the mercy of that customer . . . not a great place to be, right?

When you operate from your human brain, you respond to all types of customers in the same way. Whether they are angry or not, you are not absorbing their anger, their frustration, or their fear. You are not allowing them to affect your day. And you do this by observing instead of absorbing.

When you observe something, you become aware of it through careful and directed attention. In other words, you notice what is happening. When you absorb something, it becomes part of you and you become part of it, and if the situation or person is toxic, you will absorb that toxicity . . . not a good idea for living a great and amazing life.

In the animal brain, you literally become prepared both physically and psychologically to run or fight. The most significant and dramatic changes take place—like rapid breathing, dilated pupils, sharpened sight, quickened impulses, and increased energy to scan and search your environment "looking for the enemy." We overreact at the slightest comment. Our fear is exaggerated and our thinking distorted because we see everything through the filter of possible danger—fear becomes the lens through which we see the world.

From this animal brain perspective, our heart is closed, and we are focused on short-term survival instead of the long-term consequences of our beliefs and choices. When we operate from the animal brain, our life becomes a series of emergencies and we live from crisis to crisis. We lose the ability to relax and enjoy the moment. Again, it is important to say that the animal brain makes a great servant. The surge of adrenaline that survival mode creates is the force responsible for mothers lifting cars off trapped children and firemen heroically running into blazing houses to save people. The problem is that most of the time we do not need to defend lives or save people from burning. Most of the time our lives are quite safe and our environment is not toxic.

When the animal brain activates, however, we end up aggressive and hypervigilant, and we overreact to everything. It leads to stress, chronic fatigue, depression, and susceptibility to infection and auto-immune diseases like rheumatoid arthritis, lupus, and allergies. Sometimes we experience tension in our muscles or headache, upset stomach, racing heartbeat, deep sighing, and poor concentration. Sometimes the stress shows itself in teeth-grinding or eye-twitching.

Conversely, when you activate the human brain and observe your life, you recognize these symptoms as operating from your animal brain and living in survival and fear mode. You realize, "Wow—I am fed up with all this 'emergency' reaction way of living." And that's when you can begin to operate from your human brain. You can observe your external environment and if necessary take action to make it safer. You can work to get out of toxic, noisy, or hostile environments. You can work at surrounding yourself with friends and people who genuinely care for you. You can learn new skills to give you more responsibility over your life, such as time management, communication, or leadership skills. It's like the old proverbial saying, "When life gives you lemons, make lemonade." Without absorbing the negative energy of a person or situation, you can stand back, observe, and begin to make changes.

Being an observer does not mean that you do not take action. In fact the reverse is true. Being an observer means you take different action than you would as an absorber. An absorber tends to feel terrible because they have absorbed all the negative energy—all the anger, upset, and emotionality of a situation or person. This is not the way to live an outstanding life. So how do you become an observer instead of an absorber? We know of a couple of effective ways, quite different from each other. Both require that you take action to redirect and neutralize the energy.

Redirect with Physical Exercise

When your animal brain triggers the fight or flight response, you suddenly have a lot of energy at your disposal. If it is not used up, it can lead to an excessive buildup of stress hormones, which is not good for your body or mind. Well, believe it or not, just five minutes of exercise will effectively counteract these ill effects. Get rid of your pent-up energy by doing a few jumping jacks, push-ups, running in place, or yoga stretches. If it sounds too bizarre, then think of the alternative—tension headaches, irritability, frustration. It's your choice.

Yes, it's true: some people have it easier than others. A manager, for example, can close the door to his office and do 25 quick push-ups without anyone noticing. If you are in general view of everyone, you have to be more creative. For example, you may have to run up and down some stairs or go for a brisk walk around the building. You will return to work clearer and calmer.

Exercise increases your natural endorphins, which helps you feel better. And when you feel good your thoughts are clearer and it's easier to access your human brain. When you're tired and physically rundown, you tend to focus on what's not working, just like a cranky child who needs a nap—it's hard to be positive while exhausted or physically out of condition or sleep deprived. So for those of you who are reading this and thinking, "Easy for you to say!" just do it anyway. Try it out the next time you feel stressed. Do something physical for five minutes and feel the positive results!

Redirect with Mental Exercise

For those of you for whom physical exercise is not a possibility, you can redirect the negative energy by using a mental exercise like meditation or prayer. If possible, sit up straight in your chair and take a couple of deep breaths. Imagine yourself relaxing and say to yourself in your mind, "My toes are relaxed. My feet are relaxed. My knees are relaxed . . ." Work your way up to your head and say, "My face is relaxed. My tongue is relaxed. My eyes are relaxed. My ears are relaxed. My mind is relaxed. The hair on my head is relaxed . . ."

At this point you may already feel the benefits and don't need to go further. But if not, you can take it one step further and imagine yourself in a beautiful place—beside a lake, under a shady tree, in a meadow—wherever you feel most comfortable, and simply allow your mind to rest in that place for a couple of minutes.

This visualization process does not take long, and you will immediately feel the benefits. It begins with the breath. By slowing down your breathing you are kicking in the human brain and accessing the calm, peaceful place from which the human being operates. The animal brain cannot access this place since it is constantly talking to you and reminding you about everything you need to be worried or upset about. Don't listen—pay it no attention—tell it that you will listen later and that for now you're doing something very important for your survival! It will understand that.

Finally, a note on being the observer. If this feels unnatural to you or too strange to consider, think of it as being a witness, especially if you are operating from your animal brain and the fight or flight syndrome has been activated. Think of yourself as witnessing the event. It has nothing to do with you—you are simply an onlooker—and though you're noticing everything that is going on and listening to everything being said, you are not absorbing any of the words. They are flowing over you, and when they finally stop, you can step in and help find a solution coming from your human brain.

The human brain wants to be of service. It wants to make the world—your world—a more peaceful place, a more exciting place without all the tension. A place where you can do a great job, communicate without losing sight of who you are, and enjoy a fulfilling life. Be authentically you, the human being who wants to shine your light and be the amazing person that you already are.

Chapter Eight

MAKE STRESS WORK FOR YOU IN YOUR LIFE

I've experienced many terrible things in my life, a few of which actually happened.

—Mark Twain

Handling Stress

Everyone experiences stress, and if you're not handling stress in a positive way, your customers, family, and friends will suffer. According to the American Institute of Stress, 75 to 90 percent of all visits to primary-care physicians result from stress-related disorders. Every year, Americans cope with stress by consuming 5 billion tranquilizers, 5 billion barbiturates, 3 billion amphetamines, and 16,000 tons of aspirin (not including ibuprofen and acetaminophen).

Stress is also one of the biggest destroyers of memory. When you're stressed, you release high levels of cortisol into your bloodstream. One of the ways cortisol affects you is by destroying glucose, which is the brain's source of food. And if your brain is not getting the nutrients it needs, it will not function well.

In this chapter we will discuss not being over-stressed, even when you're living in a stressful world. Here's an e-mail we got from one participant who definitely had been going through a lot of stress in his life:

> I *don't want to beat a drum about my life's tribulations, and I want to tell you the following*: By the *time I attended your seminar, I'd had four heart attacks, and I am now surviving cancer as well as dealing with some other minor problems. I realize that I am* TRULY AMAZING, *and if you had not told me to look in the mirror and tell myself that every day, I am not sure where I would be. I tell myself every morning when I get up and every evening when I go to bed. Why? Because I* AM AMAZING. *Thanks for helping me know that.*

One of the pioneers of optimistic autosuggestion was French psychologist Émil Coué (1857–1926), who helped cure hundreds of patients using the following formula: "Every day, in every way, I'm getting better and better." (Incidentally, a similar line appears in John Lennon's song "Beautiful Boy": "Every day, in every way, it's getting better and better.")

To not believe in autosuggestion would be like saying, "I don't believe the Earth is round." Everything begins with a thought, and if you are in your animal brain, the thought is based on fear and survival. In your human brain, the thought is based on love. Like this father who wrote us:

> Everything is just great. I woke up today rocking and rolling. I had my kids rocking and rolling. We were all amazing and still looking and feeling amazing. I open myself to receive the good life has to offer.

Every day in every way people are overcoming their stresses, like this man who wrote:

> Hi, I'm doing fine, in spite of completing a move to a new house last week that wasn't quite finished, needing a new transmission in a brand new car, and my mom falling down and breaking three vertebrae in her neck (she's now in a halo ring). It was a difficult week, yet somehow I'm still smiling. It's good to be back at work.

Yes, sometimes work can seem like a vacation when there's a lot going on at home! And then there are people who have a fight on their hands, like this lady who writes: "Yes, I am still amazing. I really fight the animal sometimes, but to date I have won!"

Isn't it interesting how we get into a *fight* with the animal brain? And then, of course, what do we have on our hands? That's right—we have an actual fight with someone! So what about this: let go of the fight and begin to be in communication with your animal brain. Remember, it is there for your survival. It makes a great servant and a lousy master. You have to tell it exactly what you want: "Today I am amazing, I am going to finish the project, and tonight I am going to exercise."

When people are out of communication with their animal brain, the animal brain takes over. It becomes the master: "I'm never going to finish the project, and I won't have time to do the things I want to do." This leads to stress, unhappiness, and frustration.

If you are in a fight with your animal brain, some days you'll win and some days you'll lose—but when you do win, you're still in a fight. It would be the same as giving an instruction to an undisciplined child: "Please, just for today I want you to be great with everyone you meet." And the child replies, "No!" Then what do you do? You resort to either stating it in stronger language, yelling, being angry, or cajoling: "Please! Do this one thing for me, and I will do something for you." It doesn't work because you end up out of control and feeling bad.

Remember, the animal brain is very simple. It knows two things: fear and survival. Once you are in charge by affirming your day in a positive way, it can relax. "Okay, the boss is in charge—I can go to sleep and not stress out."

20 Ways to Make Stress Work for You

To help you deal with stress, here are 20 surefire ways to make stress work for you in your life:

1. Every time the animal brain talks to you in a negative way, say, "Thank you, not today. Today I am being amazing."

2. When the animal brain starts looking into the past and reminding you of things you could have done differently, say, "Thank you, I am now living in this new and creative moment—the past is old and gone."

3. If the animal brain starts being envious of other people, switch to your human brain and remind yourself of how amazing you are.

4. When it seems you are not good enough for the task at hand, switch to your human brain and remind yourself of all your talents, such as reading, writing, bicycling, swimming, walking,

talking, knowing two languages, being empathetic, having a friend who cares for you, being able to smile, and so on. Remember: not everyone can do or has all these things.

5. When life gets tough and you're having problems in an important relationship, remember that two animals fighting is not a pretty sight. Remind yourself that you are bigger than this. You can switch to your human brain and be amazing . . . this is your life . . . do you want to be right or let go of your fears and live a long and happy life with this other person?

6. If you think your stress level is going through the roof, you may need to talk to someone about it. Are you given too much work to handle? Is this the right job for you? Remember, you always have options. This is your life and you are in charge of it—no one else.

7. Misery loves company. If you're hanging around miserable people, you are simply feeding your misery. A miserable person does not want to be with happy people. If you have to be miserable in order to be friends with a certain person, maybe you should consider getting new friends.

8. Happiness is infectious. If you hear people laughing, it is hard not to smile. If you find yourself being sad . . . look for a good joke. To start you off, here's one that a Columbian friend told me:

El Vaquero (the Mexican cowboy) and his Chihuahua, Chilito, are camping in the desert. He sets up their tent and both are soon asleep. Sometime later El Vaquero wakes his faithful friend. "Chilito, look up at the sky and tell me what you see."

Chilito replies, "I see millions of stars, señor."

"What does that tell you?" asks El Vaquero.

Chilito ponders for a minute. "Astronomically speaking, it tells me there are millions of galaxies and potentially billions of planets. Astrologically, it tells me that Saturn is in Leo. Chronologically, it appears to be approximately a quarter past three. Theologically, it's evident the Lord is all-powerful, and we are small and insignificant. Meteorologically, it seems we will have a beautiful day tomorrow. What does it tell you, señor?"

El Vaquero is silent for a moment, and then says, "Chilito, you pendejo. Someone has stolen our tent."

9. If life is getting too serious and you're hauling around a lot of garbage, there's just one thing to do—let go of the handle. That's right, let go. Some of you might be thinking, "Easy for you to say, you don't have my life! I have commitments, people I'm responsible for." We're not saying to let go of your commitments or leave your home and never come back. What we're saying is let go of the garbage. If you owe people money, for instance, stop dragging the problem around— call them up and set up a payment plan. (I did that once, and people were amazed that I called them, and then appreciative that I had, and we worked out a plan.) Whatever the problem is, deal with it. If you're not talking to a family member or friend, call up and apologize . . . be the bigger person . . . life's too short. If not now, when are you going to let it go?

10. Carl Jung said, "I am not what happened to me; I am what I choose to become." If you are choosing to become stressed out, then you can handle it by choosing to become something different. First, realize that it is your choice. Second, make a choice to be different. Third, decide a different way of being. And fourth, do something about it. A guru once said, "If you

want to accomplish your dreams when you retire, take action today. If you want a beautiful garden, pull up a weed every day. If you want to travel, buy a map and start making plans! If you want to own your own business, begin by making a business plan."

11. The definition of *stress* is importance, significance, urgency, and weight. Are you giving certain things too much importance? Ask yourself, "When I lie on my deathbed am I going to be ecstatic that I gave this project so much importance?"

12. The opposite of stress is relaxation, calm, and comfort. If things get too stressful and you can't take a physical vacation, take a mental one! Close your eyes and imagine yourself at your favorite vacation spot (if you don't have one, you really do need a vacation). Medical research suggests that people who take regular vacations are at less risk of heart disease.

13. Take a minibreak. Even walking down the hallway will get your oxygen and blood flowing.

14. Possible thought: junk food feeds junk thoughts! Okay, so once in a while you want a doughnut. That's fine . . . just not every day.

15. Develop an after-work ritual like meditation, shooting basketball, running, or bowling— and if you are in survival mode and have to get home to look after your kids, then do something with them. Walk to the park with them. Or be honest with your partner: "Honey, would you help me wind down and come for a walk with me?" It's better than the alternative, "Would you please stop the noise— you're driving me crazy!"

16. You're perfect just the way you are, and you can let go of some things that aren't important. Brushing and flossing are important; cooking a gourmet meal every night is not. Wearing clean clothes is important; wearing expensive clothes is not. Smiling is important; watching your favorite TV program is not . . . okay it may be, but only if you smile about it. You don't want everyone in your household scared to death that you'll miss your favorite program!

17. Don't stress yourself out finding time to take a time management course; just be on time and do the things you have to do.

18. Reward yourself. There's an old adage about money—pay yourself first. Pay yourself 10

percent of your earnings before you pay anyone else. The same goes for rewards. Reward
yourself first before you reward anyone else.
Do something that "floats your boat," whether
it's taking time to go to a movie or meeting a
friend for dinner. Whatever it is, give yourself
the reward, and from that space you'll be able
to reward others.

19. Sometimes stress looks like a big mess of
chaos in your head. To counteract this, begin
with one small step. Clean your work space,
for instance.

20. Sometimes when we change, the universe
steps in and gives us a little nudge: "Are you
sure you want to do this? Are you willing to
have faith? Are you going to be happy now?"
And if the answer to any of these questions is
no, then the song goes flat. You are the singer
of your own song, and when you sing out
strong and clear, the universe steps in to
make it truly "one song." So sing in the shower and start your day with a song.

Chapter Nine

HOW TO COMMUNICATE USING ALL YOUR SENSES

Worry is a misuse of the imagination.

—Zig Ziglar
author and motivational speaker

Being Open-Minded

Communication is a mindset, and customer service is a mindset. When you are open-minded, willing, and enthusiastic, you can communicate with anyone on the planet, even the people you may not like. So we need to look at how to keep an open, clear mind. Remember, "It's not what you say, it's the way and how you say it." Included in this chapter is how to use all of your senses so you can communicate and be able to give amazing feedback to customers, colleagues, and coworkers.

On that note, we love to get feedback too. In fact, at the end of the motivational e-mails we send out each month, we ask for feedback, like this e-mail we sent recently:

Hi____,

Do you remember the Marty story in the introduction to the Super Service book? He's the tollbooth operator who decided to make a difference in his life and in the lives of other people. You see, it's not about your job, your customers, your coworkers, your partner, your children, the weather, money concerns, health problems, or any of these things. What your life is about is YOU choosing to have a GREAT life. It's your choice if you wake up happy or unhappy, depressed or full of joy—your choice, no one else's. Remember it's about switching from your animal brain to your human brain and being an amazing human being—for yourself! You deserve to have a great life—we live in an amazing country! Compared to some parts of the world, we live like kings and queens. We have hot and cold water that comes out of the wall so we can take a shower; gorgeous, comfortable beds to sleep in; food as ripe and plump and tasty as you could ever imagine, and if you don't want to be bothered to cook it yourself, you can go to a place and for a few dollars buy it already cooked! We have the best life and we deserve to be happy and filled with joy. So please let me know how you are doing.

All the very best, Jeff

Words Are 7 Percent of Communication

As you can see, the above communication is transference of information via e-mail. It's very difficult because there is no tone of voice, no physiological signs to read, just words, and as determined in the University of Pennsylvania study we mentioned earlier, words are only 7 percent of communication. Of course, there are always exceptions to any rule. Some people date via Internet, get married, and are now living an amazing life as a result of the Net . . . and at some point you have to get off the Net and jump into your life.

To communicate using all your senses, we first need to realize how many senses we have. Typically, people refer to five senses: sight, touch, taste, smell, and hearing. Interestingly, research has uncovered that when people shop for things, they like to touch what they're going to buy—hence the signs "Do Not Touch" in shops, which is why more wily shop owners have sample products for people to touch!

Then there's smell. I learned this the hard way. I was consulting with a large benefits company, wearing what I thought was a very flattering, flowery perfume, when the lady next to me said quietly in my ear, "Is that Paris?"

"Yes," I replied.

"It's a lovely perfume," she said, and then I waited for the other shoe to drop . . . which it did. "Unfortunately I'm allergic to that perfume. Would you mind not wearing it again to our meetings?"

"Absolutely," I said. It was a great piece of information, and I continue not to wear overpowering perfume in any corporate environment.

Then there's hearing. Have you ever heard a presentation made by someone who isn't speaking up? Where you have to lean forward to hear? Or conversely, where the speaker shouts and you just want to leave the room? Or the boring speaker with a flat monotone voice with little or no emphasis? To be heard, you have to speak up, be interesting, and of course have something worthwhile to say.

Then there's sight. It's a true saying, "You only get one chance to make a first impression." Of course, most people think it's all about dress—well it is and it isn't. A wise teacher once told me, "Most people think they give their business card to a person and that says everything about them—they don't realize that just by walking into a room we are instantly communicating everything there is to know about ourselves." It's true. The way we walk, shoulders back or drooping forward, head held high or looking down to the ground, swaggering and overconfident or purposeful and steady . . . all these things instantly convey the kind of person we are.

Point of View

People will instantly put you in a box depending on their point of view. If polished shoes are important to them and yours are scuffed, you'll have a hard time convincing them that you're someone who will take care of details. The way you dress tells a lot about yourself. One founder and CEO of a high-tech company had his hair in a long ponytail and wore shorts and a T-shirt every day. His company was profitable, so he could get away with it. Kind of like an eccentric and very rich person who can get away with things. Not everyone can! So you be the judge of where you are on that particular ladder.

It's being the observer, not the absorber. The observer can remove herself from the situation and not take things personally. The absorber literally absorbs what's going on and can't see herself apart from the situation. When I allow myself to observe, I can use more than my ordinary five senses; I can feel and use my intuition.

Intuition

Intuition is an amazing force that is underrated. It is the knowing without the knowledge. In other words, we simply "know" if something is right or wrong. Is this the animal brain or the human brain, do you think? Well, the animal brain has instincts—but that is not the same as intuition. Intuition operates at a human being level. It comes from being the observer, not the absorber. It uses all the five senses plus something else—that gut feeling, or that little pulse of energy that comes from the heart that says, "I don't know why, I just think this is the right thing to do."

It's that feeling you get when someone is saying all the right words yet not looking you directly in the eye, so you feel something is not quite right. Or that feeling when someone is so enthusiastic and passionate about the project that you feel: "Yes, this is worth taking a chance!"

One company we worked with asked us to help them develop a recruitment program—something that would enable them to select the right people for the job. We spent weeks with "subject matter experts," putting together job specifications and competencies from which we developed recruitment tactics, interviewing techniques, and behavioral strategies. And we do need these things to help us determine who is right for the job. But intuition is still *key* to hiring people.

Imagine how many more marriages would work if people were able to become the observer and really take a look at the person they have fallen "head over heels" in love with? I always remember a wise teacher being asked a question by a young woman in the audience: "I have been going out with my boyfriend for four months and we want to get married. I am worried because he seems to have a drinking problem and I'm not sure what to do." She looked down before adding, "I really love him, though."

The teacher looked at her for a moment and asked, "What is his name?" I thought, at the time, what a strange question to ask. Because what has a name got to do with anything?

She answered, "His name is George, but everyone calls him Dog!"

Again the teacher looked at her a moment before saying, "We can often tell what is going to happen in the future by the actions people have taken in the past. You might want to think twice about someone who has earned the nickname 'Dog' and has a problem with alcohol."

The young woman unhappily nodded her head. She'd been hoping for a different answer, even though her intuition had already told her it wasn't going to work.

ARE YOU ATTUNED TO YOUR INTUITION?

Here's an exercise to see if you are fully attuned to your intuition. You'll need to have another person to work with because you are going to use your intuition in a normal, everyday type of conversation. Got someone in mind? Good. So next time you're with them, face-to-face, here are the steps for you to follow:

1. Switch to your human brain and attune yourself to your intuition.

2. Listen to him as an observer. Is he excited or unenthusiastic? What is his body language telling you? Does his tone of voice match his words?

3. How does what he is saying affect you? Do you feel uplifted by the conversation or depressed? How do you feel as an observer?

ARE YOU ATTUNED TO YOUR INTUITION? (CONT.)

4. Is he often this way, or is he behaving out of character?

5. What does your intuition tell you about this person?

6. Share your feelings with the person and then be curious. Inquire about how he feels. It could be something like: "I noticed that when you were talking about whether to buy a new condo or not, I felt really excited for you. Is that how you feel?" Or, "When you talked about your new job, I got this feeling of stress . . . is it very challenging?"

Intuition takes listening skills to a whole different level, especially with customers, coworkers, friends, and family. Instead of listening for a break in their story so you can tell yours, listen intuitively for what is not being said. What is their tone of voice telling you? What is their body language saying? This is very useful in customer service situations because people often leave out the most important thing on their minds.

Visits to the doctor are a good example of this. You have some small thing bothering you and you make an appointment to go see the doctor. The doctor takes care of the problem, and then you ask the nagging question that has been a concern for a long time but that you haven't dared ask in case the answer is something terrible: "Doctor, I have this little lump here—I don't think it's a problem. I wonder if you could just take a peek?"

We humans will put up with something for a long time and then suddenly can't put up with it any longer and want out! This happens in all types of relationships. There is a chronic problem that neither partner wants to talk about, because when they do it always creates an argument in which both partners are convinced they're right. So the noncommunication continues until one day someone outside the situation comes along and talks about other options—it could be another job, another relationship, or another place to live. Suddenly it's all over for them, and the person who is left behind acts surprised—as if they never realized there was a problem in the first place.

Use Intuition to Uncover Problems

If your intuition is telling you that something is wrong, communicate to uncover the problem. We once were presenting a sales training program and one of the things we asked the sales reps to do was call their customers once a week just as a courtesy to find out how things were going. We received a phone call months later from one of the sales reps who told us, "It was amazing. At first, my customers thought it was a bit strange that I was calling them just to see how things were going. After a few weeks of doing it, though, they began to appreciate my call and my 'add-on.' My business has gone up 50 percent! I've made salesperson of the month twice, and it just keeps getting better."

How about with your coworkers, your partner, your children? Do you ever ask them how things are going and then sit back and listen intuitively? There's a young couple we know who are going through a difficult time in their marriage. They have three young children, and when we met them recently the husband said to his wife, "You don't seem to like me anymore, not the way you did when we were first together."

She answered, "You were romantic back then."

Then he said, "You liked me back then."

To which she replied, "I liked you because you were romantic."

And that's why a lot of marriages fail. When two people operate from their animal brains, it's tit for tat, or "If you do that to me, I will do this to you." The animal brain is about fear and survival. It wants the easy way out, and romance is too much like hard work when you feel that the person you're buying the roses for doesn't like you. And liking someone who has stopped being romantic is also too much like hard work.

If the couple agreed to switch to their human brains, they could ignite the passion and romance they used to have. A bunch of roses, a babysitter, and a night at the theater could do wonders. A smile, a touch, a soft whisper, an endearment also works well. The problem with a lot of marriages is the same as in a lot of customer relationships—people who operate from their animal brains are not willing to switch because the very act of switching appears to be giving in: "If I act romantically and buy you flowers, you will think I am condoning you not liking me, and I am not going to condone that—so good-bye flowers."

When a couple switches to their human brains, the conversation is very different: "I loved you when I married you and I love you still today. We have three great children and I want to raise them together with you. What if we each make a list of the things that we want from each other . . ." And before you think, "what a terrible idea—he or she is going to want too much," remember that's the animal brain operating from fear. The human brain operates from love—and love is not very complicated.

Love is about respect. Love is about remembering that you want to make a good impression on this person: What did I do when we were first courting? I took care of my appearance. I bought gifts. I planned outings. I agreed more than I argued. I acted from love rather than from contempt. I remained curious about him—job, hobbies, family, life.

Substitute any relationship and it is the same. You are respectful with new customers, friends, and relationships. You bend over backward to do the right thing. You dress for success and take care of your appearance. You want their good opinion. You say and do the right things. In other words you put on a great act.

There is nothing wrong in putting on an act except when you don't realize that you are. When you start to believe your own press release that you have invented about yourself, you believe you deserve more. When you operate from your human brain, you continue to put on a great act—even when you don't feel like it; even when they don't deserve it—because you operate from love. Even when you face the most difficult things in your life, you fully engage to find solutions, resolve issues, and reset the course.

Evolving human beings realize that they can reset the course. They don't blame others . . . like the government, the company, the other people who are doing everything wrong. The evolving human being accepts responsibility for making changes—and the change begins right here with this one human being, you or me. Your purpose in life is to be happy. If you want to fight, take a kick-boxing class or tae kwon do. If you want to be happy, switch to your human brain, and instead of searching for everything that is wrong with the world, start searching for everything that's right.

GO FOR IT

Instead of saying something bad about a person—find something good to say. Here is a "go for it" exercise that will absolutely change your entire life:

GO FOR IT (CONT.)

1. Pick one 24-hour period to do this exercise.

2. The only words you will speak during this time will be words of love, kindness, compassion, and peace. Anything you say will be of an uplifting, inspiring, or motivating nature. Any questions you ask will be directed toward a positive answer or outcome.

3. Words you cannot say are in the following categories:

   a. No words to do with feeling sorry for yourself or others

   b. No negative words that make another person less than yourself

   c. No swearing or cursing

   d. Nothing discriminatory or racial

   e. Nothing about feeling tired or worn-out

4. Have a notepad and pencil with you and divide the page into two columns headed Love and Fear. Under each column make a checkmark each time you had a conversation and used positive or negative words.

GO FOR IT (CONT.)

5. Count up at the end of the day.

6. Whichever column has the more check-marks is an indicator of which brain you are operating from. Love = human brain. Fear = animal brain.

One final note: The animal brain enjoys keeping you in a fearful state, so whatever your findings, be the observer and simply notice what is going on. There really is nothing going on—you are simply evolving into an amazing human being, and that means using your intuitive knowing rather than relying on the knowledge of old beliefs.

Chapter Ten

ACCEPT YOURSELF

There are two ways to live your life, one is as though nothing is a miracle, the other is as though everything is.

—Albert Einstein

Change

We've all spent some time trying to change other people because we realize we can't change ourselves. This chapter deals with how you can make great choices in the way you handle customers, events, and people in your life. When you realize there is nothing wrong with you or them, you can start to become the solution in the amazing human interactions you have on a daily basis. By the end of this chapter you will not only realize that you have nothing to change—you'll also realize that you don't have to change other people.

One of the most difficult things about a relationship with customers, friends, coworkers, spouses, partners, or children is that we want to change them.

It's as if we're saying to that person, "You are not good enough as you are; let me show you how to be better." That's not to say that we can't improve—we definitely can, and improvement is always good. Except—and here's the catch—when the improvement becomes more than the acceptance of what already was and is.

For example, when a new product is launched—whatever it is, a car, a washing machine, software, or a piece of clothing—the inventors know that improvements will be made down the road, and they accept that. We too know that we could use some improvements down the road, yet we don't seem to see ourselves as being acceptable right now—just the way we are. Can you imagine how it would be if, every day, you launched yourself onto the world as if you were an amazing human being right now?

Believing in Yourself

Imagine if you believed in yourself as a wonderful, brilliant, and talented human being right now, today, in this very moment. What would you do? You wouldn't have anyone to blame for your condition. In fact you would be celebrating and respecting your parents for creating you just the way you are. You wouldn't be looking to change other people, your conversation would be more likely to begin with, "I woke up this morning feeling amazing. I just realized I don't have to change anything about myself; I can accept myself just the way I am."

What do you think other people would say? Well, if they were operating from their human brains also, they would probably say something like, "Wow. That is so awesome. I've always admired and respected you for who you are—it's great that you realize it too."

People who accept themselves for who they are and for their talents inspire others to be the same. Customers who feel they're dealing with a person who accepts them are more inclined to be honest about their problems or concerns. There is a kind of aura around people who operate from their human brains and come from acceptance. It makes others feel comfortable. It allows others to drop their guard and speak with truth and honesty. So here's a suggestion as to what you can do for the next seven days, and if you find it helpful, to continue doing it for the rest of your life:

1. Do this in the morning as soon as you wake up.

2. Imagine today is your last day on Earth.

3. Look into the mirror and ask yourself, "If today is the last day of my life, do I want to do what I am about to do today?"

4. If the answer is "No!" for too many days in a row, you have a choice: keep doing something you don't want to do, or change what you do.

Your work is a large part of your life. If you don't like what you're doing, then keep looking—there is no need to settle for something you don't like. In fact, when people do what they don't like, everyone suffers—you, the company, your customers, and the people you work with every day. So if you look in the mirror and answer, "No, I don't want to do what I am about to do today!" ask yourself, "What is it I want to do?"

Here's an exercise to help you find out:

1. List your greatest talents. For example, it could be talking with people on the phone (that's right, we know people who have great talent at doing that). List as many of your talents as you can think of: _____

_____

_____

_____

_____

_____

_____

_____

_____

_____

_____

_____

2. Number your talents in order of importance. For example, if teaching is your best talent, write #1 beside it. Continue to number each talent.

3. Now, pair up your talents. If teaching is #1 and gardening #2, you may want to think about finding a way to teach gardening. Or if selling is #1 and sailing is #2, you may want to think about selling boats.

4. If you have reached this point and have listed no talents, your animal brain has taken over. Everyone is talented at something. You need to switch on your human brain and open your mind and your heart to the possibility that "I can live each day as if it's my last and create wealth doing what I love to do."

Chapter Eleven

EVERYTHING STARTS WITH YOU

Vision is the art of seeing things invisible.

—Jonathan Swift

Shine Your Light

Customers expect you to know your product and your services. What they want from you is your knowledge, expertise, and caring. In order to give them that, you must be able to shine your light. Everything in your life starts with you making the choice to be amazing or not. You cannot control the weather, the traffic, bad management decisions, angry customers, or upset colleagues, but you can control you. You can wake up to the fact that you are an amazing human being and that you do not have to tolerate mediocrity any-more—that you can shine your light every day. Because when you shine your light, other people will start to shine theirs. It starts with you.

Take Action on Your Visions

One of the biggest challenges we human beings have is to follow through and take action on our visions and dreams. Goal setting will take you part of the way, yet the setting of goals can often take over and become the action!

We have experienced this ourselves. A couple of years ago we hired some personnel for sales and marketing. The marketing people decided we needed a new logo, new letterhead, a new corporate image, and new branding. The upshot was, we had meetings, brainstorming, and ideation sessions to make sure everyone was on the same page with our vision. Then came the printing and discussions about envelope and note page sizes, what to put on the business cards, and on and on. A few months later, when we had our new image, we were in a meeting with everyone when one of the facilitators said, "What we need is a vision."

It was one of those defining moments when I realized that visions, goals, logos, and great looking brochures are no substitute for hard work. No one has the vision that you have, and if you sit down with a bunch of people and create one, chances are they will forget it in a couple of months. Some of our biggest clients—Fortune 500 companies that have spent millions of dollars creating a vision—have outstanding core values that are printed on every employee's personal identity tag, and still people don't know what they are. We ask them in our workshop, "Who can tell me what your core values are?"

A couple of people out of a class of 50 will recite one or two of them—no one ever remembers them all—though these values are attached to them (via the personal identity tag) all day long. Another company we work with has huge, colorful posters framed and hanging in strategic places all around its offices. Each poster has the vision statement graphically enhanced, with the core values written underneath for everyone to read—and again, sadly, very few people take any notice. In fact when we questioned some of the employees about it, they said, "Oh those! We weren't involved in making those up, so they're not really ours."

For a vision statement or a core value to work, it has to mean something to the individual. In retrospect, our vision statement should have been: "To provide employees with rewarding work that will give them a good income plus benefits and stock options."

Recognize What You Feel and Think

Everything does start with you. You are the core of your experience, and what you feel and think dictates what you will do and how you'll take action. I was just on the phone with a young friend of ours who has gone through a difficult breakup of her relationship. For months she has been holding on to the fact that they once loved each other. Meanwhile, he has moved on, found a new girlfriend, and is happily getting on with his life. She said to us, "I anchored all my hopes and dreams on this man. Ten minutes doesn't go by without me thinking about him, and I am so angry that he gave up on us."

We told her to "pull up the anchor."

She replied that it was impossible to do that. She said, "I want to have really nasty thoughts about him, so that I can get over him once and for all."

So we said, "If you think all these bad thoughts about him, who is the one creating and being left with the bad thoughts?"

"Me," she said.

"That's right," we told her. "He's happily living his life, and you are left with lots of bad thoughts, like toxins whirling around your mind. Is that how you want to live?"

She said that she didn't want to live that way, so we gave her an exercise to do. It's something we learned called *Neurolinguistic Programming* (NLP).

NEUROLINGUISTIC PROGRAMMING

If you need to quickly clear away bad thoughts, experiences, or memories:

1. Read through the instructions first, then sit quietly, close your eyes, and follow the steps.

2. Visualize your brain like a vast library of videotapes and CDs storing all the memories and events of your life.

3. Go to the shelf that is storing all the events and memories associated with the name of the person you want to eliminate.

4. In your mind, take the entire collection and turn them all into old black-and-white movies.

NEUROLINGUISTIC PROGRAMMING (CONT.)

5. Now scramble all the sound and pictures so they become impossible to see or hear.

6. Next, visualize them being tossed onto a large, burning bonfire and seeing them go up in smoke.

7. Take a deep breath and know that you've just gotten rid of the entire series of unhappy events.

Heal through Listening

Later, when we talked with the young woman with the relationship demise, she gave us some feedback about how we had listened to her. "I loved the way that you said, 'I understand' when I was telling you about what was going on in my life," she said. "I really needed that, and I loved that you didn't make me wrong or make me feel bad. Thank you."

Sometimes that's all it takes—someone to listen. Customers, friends, family, and people we live and work with all have one thing in common with us: we all need to have people who will listen to us when things go wrong. It's all very well to read a book that talks about what to do and how to do it—about just switching, and everything will be okay. Sometimes, however, we just need someone to listen from his human brain so that he can show compassion and understanding, because at those times that's just what we need.

So you can be the source of someone's healing, and you never know where or when the opportunity will arise. A smile, a friendly greeting, can be the turning point in someone's day.

See Life as a Miracle

When you begin to see everything as a miracle, you open your eyes to the miracle of life as it happens in the moment, like this person who wrote us:

> I continue to affirm my day, in fact my wife does it with me every morning. I have noticed an improved attitude and an overall increase in job satisfaction. I have been enjoying conversations with my newest customers more. Prior to your training, I had felt that my days, weeks, and months were flying by.

The job is difficult, so I guess every day I came to work I was just waiting for it to be over. I was always looking ahead and neglecting the NOW. Things have slowed down, especially the weekend, and that keeps me fresh and relaxed for the workweek.

When we perceive life as a miracle, things do slow down. We take notice of what is around us, and we get the essence of living in an amazing world. The desk that I am writing on has a smoky glass top. Where did that come from? How is glass manufactured? From sand—isn't that a miracle? My laptop on which I am forming these words—what a miracle! Only a few years before, I would have been sitting at an old-fashioned typewriter without spellcheck, a thesaurus, or any of the amazing software programs that help my writing take shape.

We have so much to be grateful for. Like this person who wrote:

So many of the issues you covered in class really hit home for me. Most were things we all know and definitely need to be reminded about over and over again! I had just made a decision a few days before the class to make a dramatic change in my position at work. I was completely freaking out about it. Now I realize I need to let go of my fear of being

*brilliant, powerful, talented, fabulous, and gor-
geous. For things to change, I have to make different choices!*

Open Your Mind to the Present

The moment we name something is the moment we stop seeing it. That's why time seems to rush by the older we get. The "been there done that" statement is really saying, "I am closed to experiencing something new because I think I already know what it is all about." That way of thinking is very limiting, because in truth we have never been in this moment before. I have never been this age typing these words before, and I have typed millions of words in my lifetime . . . not these words, though. This is a first for me, and when we open our minds, things that we expected to happen a certain way happen very differently.

Like yesterday, I was having a pedicure, and halfway through I asked Tina, the girl who was work-ing on my feet, "May I have a manicure also?" She answered yes and we continued with the appoint-ment. When she started on the manicure, however, her boss told her to go and start with another person who had just walked in. In my former days I would have been an angry customer, except now I was the observer of the situation. I knew I wanted to keep in my human brain and be great, and at the same time I did not want to wait until another manicurist became available, because they all looked very busy and would not be free for another 10 minutes.

So I stood up and said to the boss, "I'd like to pay for my pedicure now."

"You don't want a manicure?" she asked, surprised.

"No thanks."

Just then the door to the salon burst open and my three-year-old grandson came bounding in and rushed up to me saying, "Nana!" with a big beam on his face. I scooped him up, said good-bye to Tina, and left the salon. It was as if someone was saying, "Good job. You stayed a human being and here is your reward!"

We Can Make a Difference

Everything starts with you, and everything in my life starts with me. As an observer, I always have the choice—animal brain or human brain! Like this lady who wrote:

> I have to honestly say that I let things get to me a
> few days after the class. I keep telling myself to
> remember how I cried all the way home that night
> talking to my boyfriend about how I wanted my life
> to change. I need to continue to have the strength
> to BE HAPPY NO MATTER WHAT HAPPENS!

Sometimes it feels like that, doesn't it? That we want to shout, "I JUST WANT TO BE HAPPY!" It's times like those that we have to remember to be grateful for what we have and that we do have the opportunity to change. And it's good to get support around us, like this person who is a support to others:

> My day is going good and I tend to stay strong
> because I have to be supporting all these reps. And
> I know that I have the power to make the difference
> and that's why I am so good at what I do. I have
> the power! Treat every customer (rep) as if it's your
> first! And I am giving it my best.

We truly do make a difference. If you think otherwise then you are denying your power in the world. The question is, do I want to make a positive difference to those around me or a negative difference? Either way, it will take the same amount of work, and later on in your life the positive difference you make creates a positive experience in your life—a positive and rewarding past. As this person writes:

The customers always get my best and I am remembering to affirm my day in the morning and throughout the day. As you know, I do KNOW I have the power to make a difference.

When it comes to having personal power, the most important thing is to get out of our own way— to stop being in our heads talking to ourselves and making things up that are not true. In the animal brain, we are powerless victims who rely on fear, anger, and survival to push through our limitations. The human animal operates from a mindset and environment in which terrorists thrive, in which victims of anger and frustration spread more terror and mayhem. To the animal brain there are no innocent people—everyone is guilty and everyone needs to pay.

In the human brain we are powerful beyond measure and our presence automatically liberates others. In the human brain we represent all that is wonderful and amazing about the evolving human being. We give of ourselves and we work toward peaceful ways to live together. The human being determines not to be terrorized and instead works toward peace, love, harmony, and understanding.

Carl Jung said, "I am not what happened to me; I am what I choose to become." Everything starts with you, and you always have a choice. You can choose to operate from your human brain or your animal brain. Choose to live from a fear-laden perspective or a love-laden perspective. Choose to be the source of your life or make sauce of your life.

Chapter Twelve

MANIFEST THE AMAZING YOU FOR YOURSELF AND YOUR CUSTOMER

Once you make a decision, the universe conspires to make it happen.

—Ralph Waldo Emerson

Beginning Your Journey

This final chapter describes the beginning of your journey to fulfill yourself. By this we mean the person you are entitled to be, which will be amazing for you and for your customers, family, coworkers, and friends.

In customer service programs, management training programs, and the like, you might well have been told what to say and do, and at the time it intellectually made sense, but you didn't really feel it. You didn't get it at the experiential level of knowing. We will avoid that here as we present a process to help you step out of your imagined fears, out of the stresses and strains of everyday life, and remember why you are on the planet. To love, be loved, and to be happy—not just occasionally, but every day—so you can switch on an amazing power to handle any situation, event, or person. This simple process only takes about 30 seconds a day.

There are so many ways to create an amazing life. Many people, however, are so caught up in the mundane aspects of just getting by that they become like automatons. You see them everywhere—like the walking dead. They never make eye contact, never look up, and never smile. It's as if they have either forgotten whatever dreams they've had or think they can share their dream with only a few people close to them. Once you open up to the possibility of evolving as a human being, you really do see miracles . . . like the miracle of dreaming.

Consider Elias Howe, the inventor of the sewing machine. For months he tried to think of a way to attach the thread to the needle. One night he dreamt he was being attacked by a group of natives who challenged him to invent the sewing machine or die. He noticed in his dream that the tip of their spears had a hole in it. When he woke up, he decided that was how the thread was going to be attached to the needle!

Positive Thought

Or what about the power of a positive thought? Did you know that the brain cannot process a negative command or statement? If you say to a child, "Be careful, don't spill your milk," as they carry the glass full of milk across the kitchen, the child has to actually think of spilling the milk so he or she can take the necessary action not to do it. And by the child thinking of spilling the milk in order not to spill it, the usual result is a spilled glass of milk!

It's the same with commands such as, "Don't forget to take the dog for a walk!" We are literally programming people to fail. And who is most often at the receiving end of this negative programming? That's right, you and I! We have to ask for what we want instead of what we don't want. And often what we want is very simple—to the human brain. The problem is, to the animal brain everything seems complicated, when it really isn't.

For example, all the music ever written consists of patterns of no more than 12 notes. All the arithmetical expressions consist of only 10 symbols. And for all the vast computations of digital computers, everything is made up of patterns of only two components. Life is actually quite simple. It is the human animal that loves to throw a spanner into the works and make it complicated!

I've written down my list of wants. I carry it in my purse, and every so often I look at it and think, "Wow, it really is amazing! Over half of these things have already come into being." If you haven't ever done anything like this before, all you have to do is put in your "sales order." Ask for what you want as if ordering it off a dinner menu. It should be that simple.

Complete the following list by writing down everything that you've ever wanted. We provide blank lines for 10 items, but you can add more if you like—as many more as you want. Don't leave anything out, because as hockey great Wayne Gretsky once said, "You miss 100 percent of the shots you don't take."

**SALES ORDER FOR
EVERYTHING I WANT**

1. _____

2. _____

SALES ORDER FOR EVERYTHING I WANT (CONT.)

3. _____

4. _____

5. _____

6. _____

7. _____

8. _____

9. _____

10. _____

Date _____   Signed _____

What happens in a lot of programs that focus on attitude, whether they concern customer service, marriage, children, health, or money, is that in discussion, there is no apparent benefit to the people who actually have to do the work. That's why it's important to write down what you want. And in your spare time, fill in the details.

For example, one of the things I wrote down on my list last year was to own a home by a lake. I never filled in the details, however, and so the first home that came up was a decrepit old place full of trash and old pieces of junk. I wanted a place that I could walk into without too much work attached. So I started to picture exactly what I wanted, and a month later it came on the market—a great house at a great price, and just what we wanted.

Ironically, as I write about this home, in other parts of the world people's houses are being torn down and they now have no place to call home. So where does that leave us? We have so much. How do we live amazing lives knowing that other people on the planet are being manipulated and used? How do we live amazing lives knowing that some of the things our country is doing may not be for the good of others on the planet? How do we live amazing lives without feeling terribly guilty about it?

The answer for me is simply this: do your best! Be the best at your work. Be the best at providing great customer service. Be the best mom, dad, aunt, uncle, brother, sister, friend, coworker, employee, or employer that you can be. And when you fall down, as it sometimes happens, pick yourself up and be your best all over again.

Do Your Best

I don't know if you've ever had the experience of not keeping your word and having to pay the consequences for your actions. I have, and it is not great. It wastes a lot of time, emotion, and energy. While there may be some things that need to be experienced to be learned, there are also certain things that can be learned by observation. We can see consequences that have happened to others throughout history and do not have to go through the experience ourselves to understand that it's not the right thing to do. So here's a short list of things that we have learned through our own experience of what will create an amazing you:

1. Keep your word.

2. Tell the truth.

3. Treat others as you would like to be treated.

Engage Your Human Brain

Here's a list of practical things you can do to engage your human brain in order to achieve these three positives and avoid the pitfalls of operating out of the animal brain:

1. Take a breath and switch to your human brain before saying you will or will not do something. The human brain operates from love, so it will only do things that support people. It will keep promises and do the things it says it is going to do. From the human brain perspective, your word is law in your universe, and it will work to support you in keeping your word. *Your animal brain wants you to look good because it operates from fear and survival. So your animal brain will say, "Yes, you can count on me" or "Yes, I will be there on time" or "Yes, I can do that." It sounds good, except the animal brain does not think of long-term consequences, planning, or what will happen if you do not keep your word.*

2. Take a breath, switch to your human brain, and tell the truth. The human brain realizes that we are all connected. It operates from love and understands that by telling the truth the universe sings in celebration of your honesty because truth is light. *Your animal brain lives in fear, and so the truth seems frightening. To the animal brain, telling the truth is akin to giving the enemy a tool that they can use to destroy you. The animal brain doesn't even realize that*

when you lie, you have to remember it, whereas when you tell the truth, there is nothing to remember—that is why the truth keeps you enlightened.

3. Take a breath, switch to your human brain, and treat others as you would like to be treated. Because the human brain operates from love, it views other people from love. Whether that love is fun, compassion, empathy, or joy, it is always looking for the best in others. The human brain knows that every human being is connected; it realizes that we all have the same kind of experiences and that is what it connects with.

Your animal brain operates from survival and sees every other human being, even family and friends, as a potential threat and as competition. The animal brain will manipulate, destroy, and treat people with contempt, anger, and frustration.

One of the most important things about manifesting the amazing you is repetition: when you create a memory, a pathway is created between your brain cells. It is like clearing a path through a dense forest. The first time you have to hack your way through the undergrowth, and if you don't travel that path again, it quickly gets overgrown and impossible to find. If, however, you travel along that path many times, it eventually becomes a footpath, which turns into a lane, and finally a major highway. It's the same with switching to your human brain. The more times you do it, the easier it gets, and the easier your life becomes as a result.

Like this person wrote us:

I got a call from a customer who had some billing questions. I told him I did not know the answer off-hand and that I would get the info and call him back. He gave me that "Well, okay, sure you will" response, like he knew I was just going to blow him off and not call him back. So I went to get the information and called him back within 10 minutes and he was really surprised to hear from me. I told him, "If you need anything else, let me know." He has called back two different times for information and said to me, "When you get a chance, please find out and call me back." Just to know he trusts that I will call him back as soon as I get the information makes me feel better about myself. Thanks for everything I got out of the class; I am changing the way that I live my life. I choose to be happy.

I know some of you are thinking, "See, I was right. Once you do something for a customer, they keep calling back!" That's right! It's called customer service. If you decide to be of service to your "sweetie pie" by making them a cup of coffee in the morning, you have to do it every morning or they will think you don't care—which, if you do stop bringing the coffee, is true, and you've stopped caring. In the environment of the animal brain, what seems like a good idea at the time soon becomes a chore. Listening to your children and helping them with homework seems good for a couple of nights, and then it becomes too much like hard work. Finding information for customers and calling them back opens the floodgates for them to keep calling!

Except—isn't that what we want? Living in the environment of the evolving human being, we want to be of service—make the coffee every morning, help our children, get back to customers and have them keep calling us for help. From the human brain perspective, to have customers actually want to call us because they trust us to get back to them with information is what we want. In the animal brain world, customers are just voices on the end of the phone to be dealt with as fast as possible and speedily sent on their way, hopefully never to come back again.

The more you switch to your human brain, the easier it gets, even when it's difficult. Like this person who writes:

You will be happy to know that I am a student teaching in fourth grade, and every day we affirm our day! I remember how amazing I am. Today is allergy season for me, so I am showing my desire to serve by showing up awake!

And sometimes if it seems too difficult, like when you read or hear some awful news, you can do what this person does:

I'm loving every day I get up and feel well and eager to start my day. And when I listen to the news, I realize how fortunate I am to live in the country that I do. We honor each other and ourselves by treating people we greet and meet every day with kindness and exuberance. This may very well make their day, you never know.

Or this person, who simply wrote us:

I have not forgotten to keep a good attitude every day and to leave my funk at the door.

And you can have fun with making your affirmations every morning, like this person, who writes:

Just a quick note to let you know I am affirming my day. I look in the mirror every morning and tell myself how amazing I am (so far no one has come with the white coats to take me away).

And sometimes people can be resistant, like this person, who writes:

I am amazing and I handle my interactions from a great place, however, the person I interact with the most doesn't feel that he is amazing. It is very difficult to make a difference in the situation. It seems to make it worse.

Sometimes when we operate from our human brain and we are full of love, laughter, and joy, it can be annoying to someone who is in the animal brain. Coming from fear and survival, it just seems too ridiculous for words to be that happy; except that is where we have to stay—in our human brain. Why dial down your happiness just so others feel comfortable around you?

Of course, you have to be aware of what is going on. Compassion, understanding, empathy, and putting yourself in others' shoes are all part of the human brain experience. Being "over the top" happy around someone who is suffering from chronic ill health or depression is not operating from the human brain.

Evolve as a Human Being

Switching on the amazing you is about operating from your human brain and allowing yourself to evolve into the amazing human being that you already are. It is about overcoming the fears of survival that the animal brain is so concerned about. It is about doing your best, taking action, living your life to the fullest and not being scared.

I was talking a few weeks ago with a young woman who lives in an apartment in Chicago. She told me, "I am so petrified of not finding a parking spot when I get home at night that I have stopped going out in the evening."

I said to her, "Why? What is the problem of finding a parking spot?"

"They're impossible to find at night, and then I have to park three blocks away and walk home in the dark." She added, "I'm really terrified of the dark."

I asked her if she ever woke up thinking about not getting a parking spot. And she told me that yes, every morning it was on her mind—not getting a parking spot. So I told her about affirming her day. I said, "Tomorrow morning when you wake up. Look in the mirror and say, 'I always find parking spots.'"

Then she turned to me and said, "I'm also afraid of being alone."

What you tell yourself is what you are creating. If you tell yourself that you're petrified of the dark, you will be petrified of the dark. And I know some of you may say, "Yes I can tell myself I am not petrified of the dark, except I *know* that I am truly petrified of the dark." That's the animal brain talking. It is concerned for your survival and so it has to be petrified of the dark. The problem is, it will create a lot of situations where you are in the dark so it can live in its environment of fear.

The animal brain wants to survive, and the only way it can do that is to create situations of fear. If the young woman created parking spots, she would not have to worry about the dark; except the animal brain *wants* her to worry about the dark—and so it feeds her worry. Worry about the dark. Worry about parking spots. Worry about being alone. Then something wonderful happened: I ran into the young lady last night and she said with a sparkle in her eyes, "I always find parking spots now." And not only that, she looks happier; she has enthusiasm in her voice; she is an evolving human being who creates miracles in her life.

One of the easiest ways to create miracles in your life is to switch to your human brain so you can evolve as a human being. Affirm your day every morning. Here are the instructions:

1. Look in the mirror.

2. Look into your eyeballs.

3. Say, "Today, just for today you and I are amazing."

Why "Today, just for today . . ."? Because if you give instructions for longer than a day, the animal brain is going to rebel and give you a lot of feedback, such as, "You can't do it for a week, that's too long; it will never work." So you make it for just one day.

Who is the *you*, and who is the I? The *you* is the animal brain, and the I is the human brain. When you affirm your day, you want to connect with both the animal brain and the human brain. And if you are wondering who the *you* is connecting with—the animal or the human brain—maybe finding out the answer to that question will come as we evolve.

Some questions cannot be answered with the limited knowledge that we have attained so far on this planet. It's a bit like getting caught up with situations and events that are happening in other parts of the world. We know they are happening, we know they are horrendous, and what are we going to do about it?

Well, here is a list of practical things you can do as you evolve into the amazing human being that you already are:

Switch to your human brain

Affirm your day every morning

Volunteer

Give donations

Recycle

Leave places cleaner than when you found them

Think and speak kind and generous thoughts of others

Have gratitude in your heart for all that you have

Pray for others in trouble

Listen intuitively

Be generous

Promote peace

Have fun

Be enthusiastic

Find a passion

Follow your heart

Evolve as a human being

Keeping to the Journey

Evolving as a human being is a process that naturally involves problems, so getting sidetracked into operating from the animal brain is to be expected. Think of it like a road trip. When you first start out, you expect to stop and get gas, to check the road map and get your bearings. And if you get lost, you don't say, "Forget it, I'm turning round and going back home." No, you keep going because the place you want to get to is worth the trip; giving up is not an option.

You will eventually get to your goal no matter what the route. Rest stops along the way are not failures; they are just pauses—lessons to be learned. It's being overwhelmed by the fear of failure that keeps people operating from their animal brains. When you've lost your way and keep getting lost over and over, the prospect of operating from your human brain and finding love and peace in your life can become intimidating. You don't want to be disappointed again, so it becomes hard to get back on track. It seems easier just to stay angry and frustrated and blame everyone else for your problems.

When you think of it as a road trip, a journey to a loving and healthier place, you just keep on driving no matter what. This has been part of our journey to write this book—a journey in which we had to walk the talk of switching to our human brains. Especially in the times when we wondered if switching really was the option for every situation. Sometimes, in the dark moments of struggling with problems of money, business, employees, kids, the struggles seemed too much to overcome. Then one day I realized that we were doing it.

We were having fewer arguments, and those we did have were small and insignificant when we switched to our human brains. And we were being of service to each other in small ways. Like this morning, for example, I woke up and Jeff was already showered and heading out the door for an early start. Before he left he said, "I love you," and planted a kiss on my cheek. He never leaves without that little ritual—and if you have no one around to say it, look in the mirror and say it to yourself. I promise you it works!

When I got into the bathroom, Jeff had set my toothbrush out with the mint paste, and a length of dental floss laid out beside it. He'd also put my towel on the small round stool beside the shower. It's great because it reminds me that he cares. And if he goes away, I always find some way to sneak a little note in his case that says, "I love you—have a wonderful meeting!" We look for ways to be of service to each other, and although it may sound just too "lovey-dovey," why not? Why not be as helpful as possible, as in love as possible, as in harmony as possible?

I had a conversation with my brother, who was telling me about a friend of his who was waiting to hear the results of a CAT scan after her operation to remove colon cancer. He said, "The surgeons will look at this picture to see if there are any 'hot spots' in her lungs or kidneys, so she is scared to death." And then he said, "I was sitting with her for two hours in the garden yesterday talking about this and that. A bit of politics, gardening, nothing really, and then she said to me, 'This has been wonderful. For a few hours I have found peace.'"

Sometimes it's just enough to be with someone and carry on a simple conversation that lays the fears of the animal brain to rest for a couple of hours. And that's all we can do: Be our best for ourselves and others. Shine our light so the dark places of fear and survival are abated, and allow the amazing human beings that we truly are evolve! We believe in you.

Thank you.

INDEX

ABOUT THE AUTHORS

This book is about how to go from average to amazing. Don't just take our word for it—here's what other people say:

> I affirm my day when I am sitting in my car before entering the building. I park way out in the parking lot to build myself up for the day, like giving myself a box of chocolates. I am being amazing every day because I do not listen to my animal brain.

> I shared the affirmation you gave to the group with my daughter who said, "This kind of personal excellence information should be taught in high school." You are right, in our daily lives we see a lot of people let their animal brains take over. I'm basically optimistic, and after the class I am now more aware of having my human brain be in control.

> I've been affirming my day and making my bed! Amazing how I now adjust my thinking to get out of the animal brain and back into the human brain—your program has been a real eye-opener.

Who Are Jeff and Val Gee?

Married for over 35 years and working in their own corporation for 20 years has given Jeff and Val the experience of balancing their business and personal relationship with fun, passion, and enthusiasm! Learning to switch has been a major part of their success; walking the talk has given them the knowledge and understanding to write and teach what they've learned.

If you've enjoyed this book and would like to hire Val and/or Jeff Gee to come speak about the Switch method at your company, please call 847-438-9366. Other requested programs include: Leadership, Team Building, Understanding People, Competitive Sales Skills, Communication Skills, and Collaboration.

Questions for Jeff or Val? Send your e-mail to jeff@mjlearning.com, val@mjlearning.com

Check out their Web site at www.mjlearning.com